PRAISE FOR FREEDOM IN CHRIST

As a Sunday School teacher for 20 years, Freedom in Christ was the best received course that I have ever taught. Participants also stated that it was the best class they had ever attended and that everyone in the church needs to take this course.

JOHN FUGATE, M.D.
Christ Presbyterian Church
Edina, Minnesota

The following comments are from participants in a Freedom in Christ seminar. The number in the parentheses after each person's professional identification indicates how many years that person has known the Lord.

This course has helped me in every possible way. It has been faith building, skill building and confidence building. I treasure both the teaching and the fellowship.
RETIRED COUNSELOR (4)

It helped me know that no one (not even my husband) can keep me from being the person God created me to be.
HOMEMAKER AND MUSICIAN (40)

This course has lifted my burdens off my shoulders. I feel renewed. It was like the Lord has spoken to me, and consequently, I feel closer to Jesus.
RETIRED MAN (18)

I feel so much closer to Jesus and I have learned so many ways to show how much He loves me. I learned the best I can be is what He created me to be: a wife and mother and to raise my children to serve and love our Lord.
HOMEMAKER (18)

It was eye opening and freeing. It put everything in perspective with tangible helps to know who I am in Christ and how to walk the walk in victory.
HOMEMAKER AND TEACHER (46)

It has helped me free up the past, so I can look to the future.
HOMEMAKER (33)

The focus on the freedom we have in Christ helped bring a new dimension to my faith.
BUSINESS EXECUTIVE (3)

It helped me realize and gave me the tools to let go of the baggage I was still carrying around after all these years.
HOMEMAKER (8)

I understood my Christian life more clearly and realized how things in my life should change; I should change.
SALESPERSON (50)

It renewed my faith, restored a positive thought process, restored God to His proper place in my life and restored a sense of significance that has been missing lately.
RETIRED COMPUTER PROGRAMMER (8)

It helped me get back my first love for Christ. It also helped me remember where I've come from and reaffirm my faith.
SERVICE MANAGER (30)

It really boosted and refreshed my walk with Christ, helped me understand the battle for my mind and emotions and confirmed to me who I am in Christ.
COLLEGE STUDENT (8)

The course reinforced biblical truths and helped me face some sin in my life.
HOMEMAKER (50)

I feel more focused on Jesus and the impact He can have on my life if I let Him.
HOMEMAKER (23)

It returned my focus to share my faith more, to pray for opportunities, to rely on Jesus more and to speak boldly in freedom.
TEACHER (49)

This course reaffirmed that God loves me. I don't have to carry this baggage around. I'm a new person who is free and I hope—no, I pray—I can serve the Lord Jesus Christ.
HOMEMAKER AND BOOKKEEPER (3)

It has grounded my faith in Christ and illuminated the truths and revealed my misconceptions about my walk with Him.
REAL ESTATE BROKER (10)

I believe it has given me a new perspective and hopefully tools to do away with my past.
BUSINESS BROKER (37)

It was a great foundation for who I am in Christ, and I am excited to dig deeper.
TEACHER (6)

It has helped me understand and appropriate who I am in Christ and understand what that means. I am renewed.
TEACHER (15)

Wonderful foundation for who I am in Christ.
MARKETING EXECUTIVE (33)

There was so much excellent insight and reinforcement of truth said in such a clearly understandable way.
CHILD-CARE WORKER (21)

It expanded my vision of God's kingdom—my part in it—and reaffirmed to me how important wholeness in Jesus is.
INTERIOR DESIGNER (10)

I have been very blessed. This course has given me such incredible insight into some of the things I face, and the Lord showed me some things in my life that He wants to minister to me. I found freedom in significant places.
GRAPHIC DESIGNER AND CHRISTIAN COUNSELOR (26)

NEIL T. ANDERSON

FREEDOM *in* CHRIST

SMALL-GROUP BIBLE STUDY

A LIFE-CHANGING DISCIPLESHIP PROGRAM

BETHANYHOUSE
a division of Baker Publishing Group
Minneapolis, Minnesota

STUDENT GUIDE

© 2004 by Neil T. Anderson

Published by Bethany House Publishers
11400 Hampshire Avenue South
Bloomington, Minnesota 55438
www.bethanyhouse.com

Bethany House Publishers is a division of
Baker Publishing Group, Grand Rapids, Michigan

Bethany House edition published 2014
ISBN 978-0-7642-1366-3

Previously published by Regal Books

Originally published in 2004 as *Beta: The Next Step in Your Journey with Christ.*

Printed in the United States of America

14 15 16 17 18 19 20   7 6 5 4 3 2 1

CONTENTS

INTRODUCTION

Jesus said, "You will know the truth, and the truth will make you free" (John 8:32). The apostle Paul wrote, "It was for freedom that Christ set you free" (Galatians 5:1). Wouldn't you like to live a liberated life in Christ? Wouldn't you like to know how to live by faith in the power of the Holy Spirit? Wouldn't you like to know why you may still be struggling as a believer, and how you can resolve personal and spiritual conflicts? Wouldn't you like to understand the battle for your mind and how that affects you emotionally? Wouldn't you like to learn how to relate to one another in love and know how Christ meets all your needs? I'm sure you would, and that is what this course is designed to do.

THE GOALS OF THIS COURSE

This course will enable you to:

- Understand God's creation, the Fall and the gospel in such a way that you can connect with your heavenly Father and integrate the life of Jesus Christ into your daily life;

- Understand the nature of the spiritual battle for your mind and equip you to overcome the temptations of the world, the flesh and the devil;

- Understand how mental strongholds are developed and how they can be torn down through your relationship with Jesus Christ;

- Be mentally and emotionally free from your past through the process of forgiving others;

- Resolve personal and spiritual conflicts through genuine repentance;

- Live by faith in the power of the Holy Spirit in order to mature and bear fruit;

- Relate to one another from the perspective of God's grace; and

- Get on the path of renewing your mind and conforming to the image of God.

Christ is the only answer for this fallen world, and His truth will set you free. Nobody can fix your past. God doesn't even do that. He makes you a new creation in Christ and sets you free from your past. This course is designed to help you appropriate what Christ has already accomplished for you. The Holy Spirit will guide you into all truth, and that truth will set you free.

—Dr. Neil T. Anderson

THE GOOD NEWS

HE WHO HAS THE SON HAS THE LIFE; HE WHO DOES NOT
HAVE THE SON OF GOD DOES NOT HAVE THE LIFE.
1 JOHN 5:12

WORD

Have you ever thought about who you really are and why you were born? Are you just a physical being who makes a living, hoping for a little pleasure in life, and then dies? Are you the person you pretend to be? If others got to know the real you, would they like you? Perhaps the following expresses how you feel:

> Don't be fooled by me. Don't be fooled by the face I wear. I wear a mask. I wear a thousand masks—masks that I am afraid to take off, and none of them are me.
>
> Pretending is an art that is second nature to me, but don't be fooled. For my sake, don't be fooled. I give the impression that I am secure, that all is sunny and unruffled within me as well as without, that confidence is my name and coolness my game; that the water is calm and I am in command, and that I need no one. But don't believe me, please. My surface may seem smooth, but my surface is my mask, my ever-varying and ever-concealing mask.
>
> Beneath lies no smugness, no compliance. Beneath dwells the real me in confusion, in fear, in aloneness. I hide that. I don't want anybody to know it. I panic at the thought of my weakness and fear being exposed. That's why I frantically create a mask to hide behind—nonchalant, sophisticated façade—to help me pretend, to shield me from the glance that knows. But such a glance is precisely my salvation, my only salvation, and I know it. That is, it's followed by acceptance if it's followed by love.

It's the only thing that can liberate me from myself, from my own self-built prison wall, from the barriers I so painstakingly erect. It's the only thing that will assure me of what I can't assure myself—that I am really something. . . .

"Who am I?" You may wonder. I am someone you know very well. I am every man you meet. I am every woman you meet. I am every child you meet. I am right in front of you. Please—love me![1]

CREATED IN THE IMAGE OF GOD

When Adam was created by God, he was alive in two ways: physically and spiritually (see Genesis 1:26-27). Being intimately connected to God gave Adam and Eve purpose and meaning in life. Adam and Eve both knew that they were:

- Significant
- Safe and secure
- Accepted

THE CONSEQUENCES OF THE FALL

A. Spiritual Death

While Adam and Eve didn't die physically right after eating from the forbidden tree, they did die spiritually (see Genesis 2:16-17). As a consequence, every descendant of Adam is born into this world physically alive but spiritually dead (see Romans 5:12; 1 Corinthians 15:21-22).

B. Mental Depravity

Paul described Adam's descendants as "being darkened in their understanding, excluded from the life of God because of the ignorance that is in them, because of the hardness of their heart" (Ephesians 4:18).

C. Emotional Depravity
- They felt fearful and anxious.
- They felt guilty and ashamed.
- They felt depressed and angry.
- They felt powerless.
- They felt rejected.

Who I Am in Christ

I Am Accepted

John 1:12	I am God's child.
John 15:15	I am Christ's friend.
Romans 5:1	I have been justified.
1 Corinthians 6:17	I am united with the Lord, and I am one spirit with Him.
1 Corinthians 6:19-20	I have been bought with a price. I belong to God.
1 Corinthians 12:27	I am a member of Christ's Body.
Ephesians 1:1	I am a saint.
Ephesians 1:5	I have been adopted as God's child.
Ephesians 2:18	I have direct access to God through the Holy Spirit.
Colossians 1:14	I have been redeemed and forgiven of all my sins.
Colossians 2:10	I am complete in Christ.

I Am Secure

Romans 8:1-2	I am free from condemnation.
Romans 8:28	I am assured that all things work together for good.
Romans 8:31-34	I am free from any condemning charges against me.
Romans 8:35-39	I cannot be separated from the love of God.
2 Corinthians 1:21-22	I have been established, anointed and sealed by God.
Philippians 1:6	I am confident that the good work God has begun in me will be perfected.
Philippians 3:20	I am a citizen of heaven.
Colossians 3:3	I am hidden with Christ in God.
2 Timothy 1:7	I have not been given a spirit of fear but of power, love and a sound mind.
Hebrews 4:16	I can find grace and mercy to help in time of need.
1 John 5:18	I am born of God and the evil one cannot touch me.

I Am Significant

Matthew 5:13-14	I am the salt and light of the earth.
John 15:1,5	I am a branch of the true vine, a channel of His life.
John 15:16	I have been chosen and appointed to bear fruit.
Acts 1:8	I am a personal witness of Christ.
1 Corinthians 3:16	I am God's temple.
2 Corinthians 5:17-21	I am a minister of reconciliation for God.
2 Corinthians 6:1	I am God's coworker (see 1 Corinthians 3:9).
Ephesians 2:6	I am seated with Christ in the heavenly realm.
Ephesians 2:10	I am God's workmanship.
Ephesians 3:12	I may approach God with freedom and confidence.
Philippians 4:13	I can do all things through Christ who strengthens me.

THE GOOD NEWS: JESUS CAME TO GIVE US LIFE!

Jesus was like the first man—Adam—in that He was both physically and spiritually alive. Unlike Adam, Jesus never sinned. He modeled for us how a spiritually alive person can live in this fallen world so long as that life is lived dependent on the Father. Jesus gave us more than an example, however; He came to give us life. He said, "I came that they may have life, and have it abundantly" (John 10:10). The Gospel of John records, "In Him was life, and the life was the Light of men" (John 1:4). Life, acceptance, security and significance are all restored in Christ.

WITNESS

How would you explain to a not-yet Christian the truth that ultimately his or her basic needs for life, identity, acceptance and security can be met in Christ?

DISCUSSION QUESTIONS

1. Consider Adam and Eve's daily life before the Fall. How was their life different from yours?

2. What was the effect of Adam and Eve's sin on our physical bodies?

3. What was the effect of Adam and Eve's sin on our emotions?

4. When do you recall becoming aware of feelings of guilt, powerlessness and rejection?

5. Which feelings do you particularly identify with?

6. What did Jesus come to give us?

7. What impact did reading the "Who I Am in Christ" list have on you?

8. Which verses were especially meaningful and why?

9. If God says something about you that doesn't feel true or match your self-perception, how should you respond? Why?

TAKING IT WITH YOU

SUGGESTION FOR QUIET TIME

Read the "Who I Am in Christ" list out loud every day. Pick one of the truths each day that is particularly relevant to you. Spend some time reading the corresponding Bible verse(s) in context and ask the Lord to help you understand His Word more fully.

THE BIG QUESTION

Before the next session, consider the following question: Suppose you are talking to someone who is not yet a Christian. How would you summarize the gospel message in a few sentences?

Note
1. Dov Peretz Elkins, *Glad to Be Me: Building Self-Esteem in Yourself and Others,* rev. ed. (Rochester, NY: Growth Associates, 1989), n.p.

A NEW IDENTITY IN CHRIST

THEREFORE FROM NOW ON WE RECOGNIZE NO ONE ACCORDING
TO THE FLESH; EVEN THOUGH WE HAVE KNOWN CHRIST ACCORDING TO
THE FLESH, YET NOW WE KNOW HIM IN THIS WAY NO LONGER.
THEREFORE IF ANYONE IS IN CHRIST, HE IS A NEW CREATURE; THE OLD
THINGS PASSED AWAY; BEHOLD, NEW THINGS HAVE COME.
2 CORINTHIANS 5:16-17

WORD

When we accept Jesus as our Savior, He changes our very nature—we are no longer people who are displeasing to God but people in whom He delights. This can be hard for some to accept because they don't *feel* any different or because of what they have believed about themselves in the past. We are assured, however, in God's Word that this happens regardless of what we feel or believe about ourselves. Place a check mark in the box next to the statement in each set that best describes you:

- ❑ I often feel that God has rejected me.
- ❑ Sometimes I think God accepts me, but there are times when He doesn't.
- ❑ I believe that God always accepts me.

- ❑ I don't feel good about myself.
- ❑ I am just an average person who tries to contribute something to life.
- ❑ I know who I am and why God created me.

- ❑ I often doubt whether I will go to heaven when I die.
- ❑ I hope that I will go to heaven when I die.
- ❑ I'm certain that I will be with Jesus when I die.

A New Creature (1 Peter 2:9-10)

When we accept Jesus Christ as our Savior, it is the defining moment of our existence. Everything changes as we pass from spiritual death to life, from the kingdom of darkness to the kingdom of God's dear Son:

- We were "formerly darkness, but now [we] are Light in the Lord" (Ephesians 5:8).

- "For He rescued us from the domain of darkness, and transferred us to the kingdom of His beloved Son" (Colossians 1:13).

- "If anyone is in Christ, he is a new creature; the old things passed away; behold, new things have come" (2 Corinthians 5:17).

- We have been grafted into Christ (see John15:1-5; Colossians 2:6-7).

- We have a new heart and a new spirit (see Ezekiel 11:19).

As Christians, we are not recognized by our natural heritage—descendants of Adam and Eve—but by our spiritual heritage—who we are in Christ. We are new creations; we have become partakers of Jesus Christ's divine nature (see 2 Peter 1:4). It was prophesied in the Old Testament that believers would receive a new heart and a new spirit (see Ezekiel 11:19). The moment we were born again, we inherited a whole new core identity. At the very heart of every believer is a new seed of life that is waiting to take root and sprout in righteousness.

Alive in Christ

Read the list on pages 14-15 aloud as a group.

A Saint, Not a Sinner

If you have received Jesus as your Lord, you are not a forgiven sinner but a redeemed saint. The moment you became a Christian, your core identity, or who you really are deep down inside, changed from someone who was excluded from God to someone who is accepted, secure and significant in Christ.

A Whole New Person

If you think of yourself as a forgiven sinner but still a sinner, what are you likely to do? Sin, of course! In order to live a truly righteous life, you would have to be a new creation in Christ; and God has already accomplished that for you.

In Christ

Since I Am in Christ

Matthew 5:13	I am the salt of the earth.
Matthew 5:14	I am the light of the world.
John 1:12	I am God's child.
John 15:1, 5	I am a branch of the true vine, a channel of Christ's life.
John 15:15	I am Christ's friend.
John 15:16	I have been chosen and appointed to bear fruit.
Romans 6:18	I am a slave of righteousness.
Romans 6:22	I am enslaved to God.
Romans 8:14-15	I am a son (or daughter) of God.
Romans 8:17	I am a joint heir with Christ, sharing His inheritance with Him.
1 Corinthians 3:16	I am God's temple.
1 Corinthians 6:17	I am united with the Lord and one spirit with Him.
1 Corinthians 12:27	I am a member of Christ's Body.
2 Corinthians 5:17	I am a new creation.
2 Corinthians 5:18-19	I am reconciled to God and am a minister of reconciliation.
Galatians 3:26-28	I am a son (or daughter) of God and one in Christ.
Galatians 4:6-7	I am an heir of God since I am a son (or daughter) of God.
Ephesians 1:1	I am a saint.
Ephesians 2:10	I am God's workmanship.
Ephesians 2:19	I am a fellow citizen with the rest of God's people in His family.
Ephesians 3:1; 4:1	I am a prisoner of Christ.
Ephesians 4:24	I am righteous and holy.
Philippians 3:20	I am a citizen of heaven.
Colossians 3:3	I am hidden with Christ in God.
Colossians 3:4	I am an expression of the life of Christ because He is my life.
Colossians 3:12	I am chosen of God, holy and dearly loved.
1 Thessalonians 1:4	I am chosen and dearly loved by God.
1 Thessalonians 5:5	I am a son (or daughter) of light and not of darkness.
Hebrews 3:1	I am a holy brother (or sister), partaker of a heavenly calling.

Hebrews 3:14	I am a partaker of Christ . . . I share in His life.
1 Peter 2:5	I am one of God's living stones and am being built up as a spirit house.
1 Peter 2:9	I am a chosen race, a royal priesthood, a holy nation, a people for God's own possession to proclaim the excellencies of Him.
1 Peter 2:11	I am an alien and a stranger to this world in which I temporarily live.
1 Peter 5:8	I am an enemy of the devil.
1 John 3:1-2	I am now a child of God. I will resemble Christ when He returns.
1 John 5:18	I am born of God and the evil one cannot touch me.
Exodus 3:14; John 8:58; 1 Corinthians 15:10	I am not the great I AM, but by the grace of God, I am who I am.

THE FULL GOSPEL

- **"You don't know what's been done to me."** It doesn't change who you are in Christ.

- **"You don't know how bad I've been."** It doesn't change who you are in Christ.

- **"You don't know what failures I've had as a Christian."** It doesn't change who you are in Christ. Christ loved you when you were still a sinner. That hasn't stopped now that you're His.

- **"But what about my future sins?"** When Christ died once for all our sins (see Romans 6:10), how many of your sins were yet to be committed?

- **"Wouldn't I be filled with pride if I believed all those things about myself?"** Your new identity in Christ is not something you have earned. It's a free gift made possible by the grace of God alone. You are not saved by how you behave; you are saved by how you believe.

DISTINGUISHING CHRISTIANITY FROM FALSE RELIGIONS

Many find it helpful to speak the following declarations about God:

The Truth About Your Father God

I renounce the lie that my Father God is	I choose to believe the truth that my Father God is
Distant and disinterested	Intimate and involved [see Psalm 139:1-18]
Insensitive and uncaring	Kind and compassionate [see Psalm 103:8-14]
Stern and demanding	Accepting and filled with joy and love [see Zephaniah 3:17; Romans 15:7]
Passive and cold	Warm and affectionate [see Isaiah 40:11; Hosea 11:3-4]
Absent or too busy for me	Always with me and eager to be with me [see Jeremiah 31:20; Ezekiel 34:11-16; Hebrews 13:5]
Impatient, angry and rejecting	Patient and slow to anger [see Exodus 34:6; 2 Peter 3:9]
Mean, cruel or abusive	Loving, gentle and protective [see Jeremiah 31:3; Isaiah 42:3; Psalm 18:2]
Trying to take all the fun out of life	Trustworthy and wants to give me a full life; His will is good, perfect and acceptable for me [see Lamentations 3:22-23; John 10:10; Romans 12:1-2]
Controlling or manipulative	Full of grace and mercy, and He gives me freedom to fail [see Luke 15:11-16; Hebrews 4:15-16]
Condemning or unforgiving	Tenderhearted and forgiving; His heart and arms are always open to me [see Psalm 130:1-4; Luke 15:17-24]
A nit-picking, demanding perfectionist	Committed to my growth and proud of me as His beloved child [see Romans 8:28-29; Hebrews 12:5-11; 2 Corinthians 7:4]

I AM THE APPLE OF HIS EYE!
[See Deuteronomy 32:9-10.]

WITNESS

What Adam and Eve lost in the Fall was life; Jesus came to give us life. People don't like to be judged, and thus calling them sinners may be counterproductive to what you are trying to accomplish. Pascal said there is a God-shaped vacuum in every person. People *need* new life in Christ. How might knowing that help you in witnessing to others?

DISCUSSION QUESTIONS

1. To what degree have you struggled with a negative self-image?

2. What caused you to feel that way about yourself?

2. Have you understood yourself to be a sinner or a saint? What or who contributed to that assessment?

3. Why is it so important to understand the whole gospel?

4. What should we do when we sin?

5. What has been your perception of God in the past, and what contributed to it?

6. What is your perception now? Why?

TAKING IT WITH YOU

SUGGESTION FOR QUIET TIME

Read the entire "In Christ" list out loud every day this week. Look up each verse in your Bible and read it. Then do the same for the verses revealing the truth about God.

THE BIG QUESTION

Before the next session, consider the following question: How does a Christian walk by faith?

Note: For additional help, read Neil T. Anderson and Dave Park, *Overcoming Negative Self-Image* (Ventura, CA: Regal Books, 2003).

LIVING BY FAITH

WITHOUT FAITH IT IS IMPOSSIBLE TO PLEASE HIM, FOR HE WHO
COMES TO GOD MUST BELIEVE THAT HE IS AND THAT HE IS A
REWARDER OF THOSE WHO SEEK HIM.
HEBREWS 11:6

WORD

Relativism is the predominant philosophy in our postmodern world. In contrast, Christianity asserts that God is the ultimate reality and that His Word is absolute truth. Creation cannot determine what is true and what is real; only the creator can do that. Truth is something we choose to believe or not, and choosing to believe what God says is true is the only means by which we can live a righteous life.

Complete the following sentences:

· Faith is . . .

· I would have more faith if I . . .

· The difference between the Christian faith and the faith of other religions is . . .

· I live by faith when I . . .

The Essence of Faith

A. Faith Depends on Its Object (See Hebrews 13:8)

   The only difference between Christian and non-Christian faith is the object of our faith.

B. The Measure of Faith Depends on Our Knowledge of the Faith Object (See Romans 10:17)

   If you have little knowledge of God and His ways, you will have little faith.

C. Faith Is an Action Word (See James 2:17-18)

   People don't always live what they profess, but they always live what they have chosen to believe. What you do is just a reflection of what you believe.

Distortions of Faith

A. New Age and Eastern Religion Philosophies

   Faith without action is one distortion, but New Age and Eastern philosophies offer another distortion of what it means to believe. These gurus teach, "If you believe hard enough, what you believe will become true." Christianity says, "It is true; therefore, we believe it." Believing something doesn't make it true and not believing something doesn't make it false.

B. The Power of Positive Thinking versus the Power of Truth Believing

   Motivational speakers understand the problem with unbelief. Henry Ford once said, "Whether you think you can or whether you think you can't, you are right." Such optimists stress the power of positive thinking. The following poem further illustrates this point:

> If you think you are beaten—you are.
> If you think you dare not—you don't.
> If you think you'll lose—you've lost.
> For out of the world we find
> That success begins with a fellow's will;
> It's all in the state of mind.
> Life's battles don't always go
> To the stronger or the faster man;
> But sooner or later the man that wins
> Is the one who thinks he can.
> —Anonymous

Twenty Cans of Success

1. Why should I say I can't when the Bible says I can do all things through Christ who gives me strength? (See Philippians 4:13.)

2. Why should I worry about my needs when I know that God will take care of all my needs according to His riches in glory in Christ Jesus? (See Philippians 4:19.)

3. Why should I fear when the Bible says God has not given me a spirit of fear, but of power, love and a sound mind? (See 2 Timothy 1:7.)

4. Why should I lack faith to live for Christ when God has given me a measure of faith? (See Romans 12:3.)

5. Why should I be weak when the Bible says that the Lord is the strength of my life and that I will display strength and take action because I know God? (See Psalm 27:1; Daniel 11:32.)

6. Why should I allow Satan control over my life when He that is in me is greater than he that is in the world? (See 1 John 4:4.)

7. Why should I accept defeat when the Bible says that God always leads me in victory? (See 2 Corinthians 2:14.)

8. Why should I lack wisdom when I know that Christ became wisdom to me from God and that God gives wisdom to me generously when I ask Him for it? (See 1 Corinthians 1:30; James 1:5.)

9. Why should I be depressed when I can recall to mind God's loving-kindness, compassion, faithfulness and have hope? (See Lamentations 3:21-23.)

10. Why should I worry and be upset when I can cast all my anxieties on Christ who cares for me? (See 1 Peter 5:7.)

11. Why should I ever be in bondage knowing that there is freedom where the Spirit of the Lord is? (See 2 Corinthians 3:17; Galatians 5:1.)

12. Why should I feel condemned when the Bible says there is no condemnation for those who are in Christ Jesus? (See Romans 8:1.)

13. Why should I feel alone when Jesus said He is with me always and He will never leave me nor forsake me? (See Matthew 28:20; Hebrews 13:5.)

14. Why should I feel like I'm cursed or have bad luck when the Bible says that Christ rescued me from the curse of the law that I might receive His Spirit by faith? (See Galatians 3:13-14.)

15. Why should I be unhappy when I, like Paul, can learn to be content whatever the circumstances? (See Philippians 4:11.)

16. Why should I feel worthless when Christ became sin for me so that I might become the righteousness of God? (See 2 Corinthians 5:21.)

17. Why should I feel helpless in the presence of others when I know that if God is for me, who can be against me? (See Romans 8:31.)

18. Why should I be confused when God is the author of peace and He gives me knowledge through His Spirit who lives in me? (See 1 Corinthians 2:12; 14:33.)

19. Why should I feel like a failure when I am more than a conqueror through Christ who loved me? (See Romans 8:37.)
20. Why should I let the pressures of life bother me when I can take courage knowing that Jesus has overcome the world and its problems? (See John 16:33.)

WITNESS

1. Think of someone you know who is not yet a Christian. What does the Bible say about why he or she does not yet believe (see Romans 10:14-15; 2 Corinthians 4:4)?

2. How can you share your faith with this person?

3. How can you pray against Satan's blinding?

DISCUSSION QUESTIONS

1. Have you ever experienced a time when you had to take God at His Word? What happened?

2. Do you agree that everyone lives by faith? Explain your answer.

3. How much faith do you think it takes to believe that the whole universe came about by chance?

4. Do you agree that who or what you put your faith in determines whether your faith is effective? Or does it have more to do with how much faith you have?

4. Do you think that we can choose to have faith? Why or why not?

5. Can you think of a time when you asked God to do something and were disappointed because He didn't answer your prayer in the way you wanted? (For example, have you ever prayed faithfully for someone to be healed, but then the person died?) What do you conclude from such difficult experiences?

6. Elijah said, "How long will you hesitate between two opinions? If the LORD is God, follow him; but if Baal, follow him" (1 Kings 18:21). What is keeping you from making a commitment to base your life solely on what God says is true, regardless of your feelings or the opinions of others?

TAKING IT WITH YOU

SUGGESTION FOR QUIET TIME

Read the "Twenty Cans of Success" list out loud every day. Pick one of the truths that is particularly appropriate to you and make a decision to believe it, regardless of your feelings and circumstances. Commit yourself to step out in faith based on the truth you have learned this week!

THE BIG QUESTION

Before the next session, consider the following question: How is your perspective of this world different from that of others and how is it different from the way God sees this world?

RESHAPING OUR WORLDVIEW

THEREFORE AS YOU HAVE RECEIVED CHRIST JESUS THE LORD, SO WALK IN HIM, HAVING BEEN FIRMLY ROOTED AND NOW BEING BUILT UP IN HIM AND ESTABLISHED IN YOUR FAITH, JUST AS YOU WERE INSTRUCTED, AND OVERFLOWING WITH GRATI- TUDE. SEE TO IT THAT NO ONE TAKES YOU CAPTIVE THROUGH PHILOSOPHY AND EMPTY DECEPTION, ACCORDING TO THE TRADITION OF MEN, ACCORDING TO THE ELEMENTARY PRINCIPLES OF THE WORLD, RATHER THAN ACCORDING TO CHRIST.
COLOSSIANS 2:6-8

WORD

The world in which we were raised has influenced our perception of reality. Consequently, we have a tendency to interpret life from a limited worldly perspective. Our worldview is a grid by which we evaluate life experiences. Wisdom is seeing life from God's perspective and evaluating life through the grid of Scripture. To change our worldview requires repentance, which literally means a change of mind.

DEFINING THE TERM "WORLDVIEW"

Our present understanding of this world was assimilated from the environment in which we were raised and developed through numerous learning experiences, most of which were informal. There is no society in which all people hold exactly the same worldview. In North America it is politically correct to have tolerance for different opinions and beliefs. The question is, How does our worldview differ from a biblical worldview? To start with, let's put on a different pair of glasses that will allow us to see in broad strokes how people interpret this world from different perspectives.

DIFFERENT WORLDVIEWS

A. Animism

Animism is the oldest and probably most widely held worldview. It is found in its purest form in preliterate, tribal societies, but some elements are found in most modern societies. Most animists believe in a creator, or god (or gods), but see their god or gods as being so far removed from them that it would be difficult to make any connection. The animist is more concerned with a neutral spiritual power (mana) that is thought to permeate everything in the universe—animal, vegetable and mineral—and with spirits of many types (see figure 4-A).

Figure 4-A

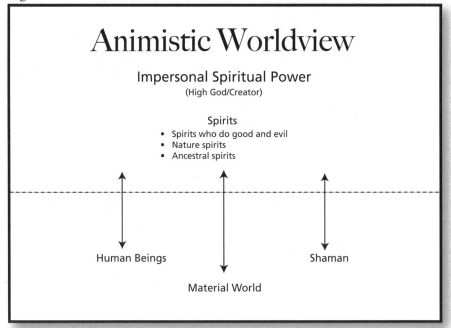

B. Eastern Religions, or Philosophies

1. In Eastern religions, there is no personal God. Instead, there is an impersonal cosmic force that permeates everything.

2. Hinduism is one of the earliest formalized religions, dating back to 1500 B.C.

3. Ayurveda (pronounced ay-yoor-va-duh) is a type of Hinduism that believes that the basis of life is rooted in the nonmaterial world, in a field of energy known as *prana*.

4. Taoism has two faces, yin and yang, which oppose each other yet are one. Human beings are said to be inseparable from yin, yang and the world about them.

MODERN WESTERN WORLDVIEW

According to the modern Western worldview, the world is generally divided into two functional realms: the supernatural realm and the natural realm as shown in figure 4-B. All spirit beings, including God, angels and demons, are placed in the supernatural realm because they don't functionally fit with the natural world of scientific rationalism. From this perspective, there is a chasm between the spiritual realm and the natural realm.

Figure 4-B

Western Worldview

(God)

Supernatural Realm of Religion

Angels and Demons

Excluded Middle

Natural Realm of Science

People

A. Rationalism and Naturalism

Rationalism and naturalism have dominated the Western culture throughout most of the twentieth century. Although most people say they believe in God, the majority do not believe that the existence of God significantly impacts their daily life.

B. Postmodernism

Rationalism and naturalism are being replaced by postmodernism as the dominant worldview in the Western world. Friedrich Nietzsche summed up postmodernism when he said, "There are many kinds of eyes. . . . Consequently there are many kinds of 'truths,' and consequently there is no truth."[1] Postmodernism doesn't differentiate between what a person thinks or does and the person himself: *Who I am is equal to what I do. If you say that my behavior is wrong, you're judging me. If you disagree with my beliefs, you're disparaging me.* Consequently, there is enormous pressure to accept everybody's lifestyle as true and valid, no matter what it is.

GOD'S WORD IS TRUE

God is the ultimate reality, and He is the truth. Logic and Christian faith are not incompatible. The rules of logic demonstrate the existence of a rational God who has revealed to humankind that which is true. Divine revelation is consistent with the natural sciences since God created all that is natural and left us with the ability to discover the natural laws that govern the universe.

THE BIBLICAL WORLDVIEW (COLOSSIANS 2:6-8)

The worldview taught by the true prophets and apostles has three functional realms: the realm of God, the realm of angels, and the realm of people and material things (see figure 4-C). These are not spatial realms but realms of being. God is not limited to a spatial realm existing far away in outer space. He is present everywhere in His creation and sustains all things by His power (see Hebrews 1:3). Jehovah God is the one and only being in the realm of deity—not God and angels, and certainly not God and Satan. Satan is a created being and does not possess the attributes of God. Satan is a fallen angel, and when he rebelled against God, he was thrown out of heaven and took a third of the angels with him.

WITNESS

1. How will understanding that we all grow up with different worldviews help you talk to people who are not yet Christians?

2. What will you say to those who regard belief in absolute truth as being narrow-minded and bigoted?

Figure 4-C

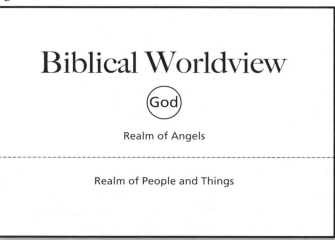

DISCUSSION QUESTIONS

1. What was the worldview that you adopted as you were growing up?

2. Which worldview discussed in this session best describes the beliefs you held prior to coming to Christ?

3. Is your Christian worldview more valid or less valid than that of someone who grew up in another part of the world? Why?

4. What measure would you use to determine whether or not someone else's worldview is true?

5. When we make a stand for what we believe to be the truth, how can we do so without coming across as arrogant?

6. How can we disagree with someone's beliefs or actions without rejecting him or her as a person?

TAKING IT WITH YOU

SUGGESTION FOR QUIET TIME

Ask the Holy Spirit to guide you into all truth and reveal to your mind the lies you have believed about the world in which we live.

THE BIG QUESTION

Before the next session, consider the following question: Paul teaches that if believers live by the Spirit, they will not carry out the desires of the flesh (see Galatians 5:16). How do believers live by the Spirit?

Note

1. Friedrich Nietzsche, The Will to Power, Book III, article 540. http://www.publicappeal.org/library/nietzsche/Nietzsche_the_will_to_power/the_will_to_power_book_III.htm (accessed February 5, 2004).

LIVING BY THE SPIRIT

BUT I SAY, WALK BY THE SPIRIT, AND YOU WILL NOT CARRY OUT THE DESIRE OF THE FLESH. FOR THE FLESH SETS ITS DESIRE AGAINST THE SPIRIT, AND THE SPIRIT AGAINST THE FLESH; FOR THESE ARE IN OPPOSITION TO ONE ANOTHER, SO THAT YOU MAY NOT DO THE THINGS THAT YOU PLEASE. BUT IF YOU ARE LED BY THE SPIRIT, YOU ARE NOT UNDER THE LAW.
GALATIANS 5:16-18

WORD

When we become Christians, we are made new creations in Christ (see 2 Corinthians 5:17); however, we will still continue to struggle with our old sin nature. As Christians, we are no longer under the Law because the Law was a tutor to lead us to Christ. Christians can live a righteous life by believing what God says is true and by living in the power of the Holy Spirit.

WALKING BY THE SPIRIT (GALATIANS 5:16-18)

How then do we live, or walk, by the Spirit? If we were to answer this question with three steps and a formula, we'd be putting Christians back under the law! To walk by the Spirit is not a legal issue—it's a personal one.

In order to understand what walking by the Spirit is, let's take a look at Galatians 5:16-18, which explains what walking by the Spirit is not. When we understand what it is not, we can then identify parameters within which we are to live.

A. Walking by the Spirit Is Not License (Galatians 5:13)

"License" can be defined as an excessive or undisciplined lifestyle that constitutes the abuse of a privilege. It is a total disregard for rules and regulations. If we choose to walk by the flesh, we will have to live with the negative consequences that come from making bad choices. Living by the Spirit, however, has no negative consequences.

B. Walking by the Spirit Is Not Legalism (Galatians 5:1; Romans 7:6)

God has called us to live righteous lives, but we cannot do that by living under the Law. There are three reasons for this.

- The Law commonly produces guilt (see Galatians 3:10-14).

- The Law is powerless to give life (see Galatians 3:21; 2 Corinthians 3:6).

- The Law has the capacity to stimulate the desire to do that which it was intended to prohibit (see Romans 7:5,8).

C. What Walking by the Spirit *Is* (2 Corinthians 3:17)

If walking by the Spirit is not license, and it's not legalism, then what is it? It is liberty. "Now the Lord is the Spirit, and where the Spirit of the Lord is, there is liberty" (2 Corinthians 3:17).

WALKING WITH GOD (ROMANS 8:14)

A. Take Up His Yoke

Jesus said, "Take My yoke upon you and learn from Me, for I am gentle and humble in heart . . . for My yoke is easy and My burden is light" (Matthew 11:29-30). When we are yoked with Jesus, He will maintain a steady pace right down the center of that narrow path, where our walk is one of faith and not of sight, and one of grace and not legalism.

B. Follow His Lead

Being led by the Spirit is defined by two parameters:

1. The Holy Spirit is not pushing us.

2. The Holy Spirit is not luring us away.

Walking by the Spirit is neither license nor legalism. It's not sitting passively, waiting for God to do something; nor is it running around in endless activities, trying to accomplish something by our own strength and resources. If we walk by the Spirit, we are neither driven nor lured off the path of faith. "For all who are being led by the Spirit of God, these are sons of God" (Romans 8:14).

WITNESS

How can being led by the Holy Spirit affect your witness?

DISCUSSION QUESTIONS

1. What were the key elements ensuring the safe landing of the young pilot in the opening illustration?

   a. Knowledge of _____

   b. Faith in _____

2. Why has simply preaching morality not changed our society?

3. What does legalism accomplish, and why is the law ineffective?

4. Has the laying down of the law in your church, home or society ever stimulated you to do what the law was intended to prohibit? Explain.

5. Which side of the road (the cliff or the fire) represents your greater weakness—license or legalism? How can you stay in the center of the road?

6. What would you learn if you walked with Jesus?

7. How did Jesus describe Himself?

8. How does the Holy Spirit's guidance come or not come, and who can expect to be guided?

9. What steps can you take to be more sensitive to the Holy Spirit's guidance in your life?

TAKING IT WITH YOU

SUGGESTION FOR QUIET TIME

Begin each day by asking your heavenly Father to fill you with His Holy Spirit, and commit yourself to live by faith in the power of the Holy Spirit.

THE BIG QUESTION

Before the next session, consider the following question: Since you are a new creation in Christ, why do you still struggle with the same old thoughts and habits?

RENEWING THE MIND

FOR THOUGH WE WALK IN THE FLESH, WE DO NOT WAR ACCORDING TO THE FLESH, FOR THE WEAPONS OF OUR WARFARE ARE NOT OF THE FLESH, BUT DIVINELY POWER-FUL FOR THE DESTRUCTION OF FORTRESSES. WE ARE DESTROYING SPECULATIONS AND EVERY LOFTY THING RAISED UP AGAINST THE KNOWLEDGE OF GOD, AND WE ARE TAKING EVERY THOUGHT CAPTIVE TO THE OBEDIENCE OF CHRIST.
2 CORINTHIANS 10:3-5

WORD

When we come into this world, we have neither the presence of God in our lives nor the knowledge of His ways. So we learn how to live our lives independently of God. In order to grow, we have to be transformed by the renewing of our minds.

RENEWING THE MIND (ROMANS 12:2)

We are no longer slaves to sin because we are bond servants of Christ. So then, if this is true—and it is—why don't we feel much different from the way we felt before we received Christ, and why are we still struggling with the same issues we struggled with before we became Christians?

MAJOR CONTRIBUTING FACTORS TO STRONGHOLDS

Mental strongholds are sometimes called flesh patterns and are very similar in concept to what psychologists call defense mechanisms. Our temperaments have been shaped by mental strongholds. It will take time to renew our minds and to replace the lies we have believed with the truth of God's Word. Most of our pre-Christian attitudes and values have been assimilated from our environment in two ways.

A. Prevailing Experiences

A major part of the programming of our worldview and attitudes took place in our early childhood through prevailing experiences (e.g., the families we were raised in, the churches we attended or didn't attend, the neighborhood and communities we grew up in, the friends that we had or didn't have) and how we responded to our environment.

B. Traumatic Experiences

The second greatest contributor to the development of mental strongholds is traumatic experiences. These experiences have been burned into our minds suddenly due to their intensity. Such trauma could include rape, divorce and death.

C. Temptation (1 Corinthians 10:13)

Temptation begins with a seed thought in our minds; and unless we take our thoughts captive, we will eventually allow them to lead us to sin.

D. Habit (James 1:15)

If we don't take that first thought captive in obedience to Christ, we will respond emotionally to our thoughts. Our feelings are primarily a product of our thought life. If we continue to act on that choice, we will establish a habit in about six weeks. If the habit persists, a stronghold will develop in our minds, becoming evident in our temperaments and in the way we live.

EXAMPLES OF STRONGHOLDS

Strongholds are habitual thought patterns. They are caused by memory traces burned into our minds over time or by the intensity of traumatic experiences. Consider the following examples:

A. Inferiority

When we continue to strive for the elusive acceptance that never comes, we begin to struggle with a sense of inferiority because there will always be someone who is stronger, smarter or better looking than we are.

B. Homosexuality

Those who are caught in the stronghold of homosexuality weren't born that way. Because of the Fall, a person can be genetically predisposed to certain strengths and weaknesses, but that does not make a person homosexual from birth. Homosexuality is a false identity with which we have labeled ourselves or others.

C. Alcoholism

Adult children of alcoholics tend to struggle with this stronghold. Suppose three boys were raised by a father who became addicted to alcohol. The older boy tried to stand up to Dad, the middle boy accommodated him, while the youngest was terrorized. Twenty years later when these boys are confronted with a hostile situation, how will they respond? The older one will fight, the middle one will accommodate and the younger one will run and hide. Those are mental strongholds.

WITNESS

1. Knowing that people have certain mindsets because of their upbringing, how might this help or hinder your witness to them?

2. Since people are in bondage to the lies they have believed, what hope could you extend to them?

DISCUSSION QUESTIONS

1. Why don't all Christians think the same?

2. How do mental strongholds develop?

3. Share an example of how believing a lie has affected how people feel about God or someone else. Can you give a personal example?

4. How can Christians stand up against temptation?

5. Why must we choose to believe what God says is true even when it doesn't feel true?

6. Explain why born-again believers may not feel saved or that God loves them.

TAKING IT WITH YOU

SUGGESTION FOR QUIET TIME

During the coming week, take time each day to meditate on the following Scripture passages:

- Romans 8:31-39

- Ephesians 1:1-19

- Philippians 4:12-13

THE BIG QUESTION

Before the next session, consider the following question: How can Satan deceive you?

THE BATTLE FOR THE MIND

PUT ON THE FULL ARMOR OF GOD, SO THAT YOU WILL BE ABLE TO STAND FIRM AGAINST THE SCHEMES OF THE DEVIL. FOR OUR STRUGGLE IS NOT AGAINST FLESH AND BLOOD, BUT AGAINST THE RULERS, AGAINST THE POWERS, AGAINST THE WORLD FORCES OF THIS DARKNESS, AGAINST THE SPIRITUAL FORCES OF WICKEDNESS IN THE HEAVENLY PLACES. THEREFORE, TAKE UP THE FULL ARMOR OF GOD, SO THAT YOU WILL BE ABLE TO RESIST IN THE EVIL DAY, AND HAVING DONE EVERYTHING, TO STAND FIRM.
EPHESIANS 6:11-13

WORD

After the Fall, humankind lost its position and relationship with God, and Satan became the rebel holder of authority over this fallen world. Jesus referred to Satan as "the ruler of this world" (John 12:31) and "the prince of the power of the air" (Ephesians 2:2), and said that the whole world lies in his power (see 1 John 5:19) because he has deceived the inhabitants of the earth (see Revelation 13:14).

SATAN THE DECEIVER

Just as God created everything on Earth, He also created the angels in heaven. One of these angels was named Lucifer, which means "light bearer." This angel reflected the light and glory of God. A very beautiful angel, Lucifer was prideful and self-centered, and he challenged the throne of God (see Isaiah 14:12-14). Because of this rebellious act, Lucifer and the angels who had sided with him were cast out of heaven by God.

THE POSITION OF THE BELIEVER

Authority is the right to rule, and power is the ability to rule. As Christians we have authority over the kingdom of darkness because of our position in Christ.

We have the authority to do God's will—nothing more and nothing less. As long as we are filled with the Holy Spirit, we have the power to do His will. "Finally, be strong in the Lord and in the strength of His might" (Ephesians 6:10).

We Are Identified with Christ
Read the following ways in which we are identified in Christ:

In His death	Romans 6:3; Galatians 2:20; Colossians 3:1-3
In His burial	Romans 6:4
In His resurrection	Romans 6:5,8,11
In His ascension	Ephesians 2:6
In His life	Romans 5:10
In His power	Ephesians 1:19-20
In His inheritance	Romans 8:16-17; Ephesians 1:11-12

Our only sanctuary is our position in Christ!

THE BATTLE FOR OUR MIND (JOHN 17:14-18)

Every Christian has experienced his temptations and accusations, but the real struggle is deception. That is why truth sets us free.

A. The Example of David
    David, a man wholly devoted to God, experienced deception when Satan moved him "to number Israel" (1 Chronicles 21:1).

B. The Teaching of Paul
    Paul voiced his concern for believers in 2 Corinthians 2:10-11; 4:3-4; 11:3 and 1 Timothy 4:1 when he wrote, "I am afraid that, as the serpent deceived Eve by his craftiness, your minds will be led astray from the simplicity and purity of devotion to Christ . . . the Spirit explicitly says that in later times some will fall away from the faith, paying attention to deceitful spirits and doctrines of demons."

C. Renewing the Mind
    The Bible teaches that we are to use our minds actively and not passively. We should focus our thoughts externally, not internally.

1. Let the peace of Christ rule in your heart (see Colossians 3:15-16).

2. Prepare your mind for action (see 1 Peter 1:13).

3. Focus your mind actively and externally.

4. Choose the truth.

WITNESS

Freeing people from demonic strongholds was the primary appeal of the gospel in the Early Church and the basis for much of the Early Church's evangelistic efforts. Since Satan has blinded the minds of your non-Christian friends, how can you be a positive witness to them?

DISCUSSION QUESTIONS

1. If Satan has been defeated and disarmed, how is he able to continue to rule this world?

2. The struggle in your mind can consist of mental strongholds, or flesh patterns, or it can be a spiritual battle for your mind. How can you tell the difference?

3. Do you need to know the difference? Why?

4. What is the difference between power and authority?

5. Which do believers have in the spiritual realm, and what qualifies them to have either?

6. Read Ephesians 6:10-18. Putting on the armor of God requires an action by the believer. What must we do to actively put on the armor of God?

7. What has already been done by Christ that we no longer have to do?

8. What is the practical difference between trying not to think negative thoughts and choosing to think upon that which is true?

9. How can you renew your mind?

10. How can you stop treading water and instead swim to shore?

TAKING IT WITH YOU

SUGGESTION FOR QUIET TIME

Meditate every day during the coming week on each of the following verses:

- Matthew 28:18

- Ephesians 1:3-14; 2:6-10

- Colossians 2:13-15

THE BIG QUESTION

Before the next session, consider the following question: If we can't always believe what we feel, how should we deal with our emotions?

EMOTIONAL FREEDOM

THEREFORE, LAYING ASIDE FALSEHOOD, SPEAK TRUTH EACH ONE OF
YOU WITH HIS NEIGHBOR, FOR WE ARE MEMBERS OF ONE ANOTHER.
BE ANGRY, AND YET DO NOT SIN; DO NOT LET THE SUN GO DOWN
ON YOUR ANGER, AND DO NOT GIVE THE DEVIL AN OPPORTUNITY.
EPHESIANS 4:25-27

CASTING ALL YOUR ANXIETY ON HIM, BECAUSE HE CARES FOR YOU.
BE OF SOBER SPIRIT, BE ON THE ALERT. YOUR ADVERSARY, THE DEVIL,
PROWLS AROUND LIKE A ROARING LION, SEEKING SOMEONE TO DEVOUR.
1 PETER 5:7-8

WORD

When God created human beings, He equipped us with a complex emotional nature. Thus far in this course we have been challenged to believe that what God says is true regardless of our feelings. This is different from denying our feelings, however, and it is important to understand that our emotions are directly affected by what we believe and how we live our life.

OUR EMOTIONS REVEAL WHAT WE THINK AND BELIEVE

In a general sense, our emotions are a product of our thought life. If we are not thinking right and our minds are not being renewed—if we are not correctly believing God and His Word—it will show up in our emotional life. If we fail to appropriately acknowledge our emotions, we may become spiritually vulnerable. For a scriptural illustration of the connection between beliefs and emotions, consider Lamentations 3.

Ways We Respond to Our Emotions

A. Suppression (Psalm 32:3,6)

   Unlike repression, which is an unconscious denial of feelings, those of us who suppress our emotions make a conscious choice to ignore them. Suppression is physically unhealthy, and it is also dishonest.

B. Indiscriminate Expression (James 1:19-20)

   Another unhealthy way to respond to our emotions is thoughtless expression of everything we feel. Instead of bottling up our feelings, we constantly blurt out how we feel without regard to those around us. This can cause major damage to our relationships with others.

C. Acknowledgment (Psalm 109:1-13)

   Acknowledging how we feel and then working to resolve the underlying problem is the key to dealing with our emotions in a healthy way. Emotional honesty begins with God.

We cannot be right with God and not be real, and if necessary God may have to make us real in order for us to be right with Him.

Responding to Emotional Honesty from Others

One of the great challenges in life is learning how to respond to others when they acknowledge their pain. It can be difficult to learn that we should respond to the pain, not the words used to express it.

A. Sharing Emotional Honesty in Relationships

   By speaking the truth in love, we are able to spend less energy fending off verbal arrows and more energy helping to find an immediate solution to the problem.

B. Knowing Our Emotional Limits

   We should be able to gauge our emotional limitations. If we are emotionally exhausted, we should not confront others or attempt to make important decisions.

HEALING EMOTIONAL WOUNDS FROM THE PAST

Traumatic experiences in our past can leave deep emotional scars. Any number of traumatic events can stay buried in our memories and remain available for instant recall. The intensity of our primary emotions is determined by our previous life history. The more traumatic the experience, the more intense the primary emotion. Notice the sequence of events:

A. Previous Life History
   Determines the intensity of primary emotions.

B. Present Event
   Triggers the primary emotion.

C. Primary Emotion
   Displays residual effect of past traumas.

D. Mental Evaluation
   Manages the emotions.

E. Secondary Emotion
   Occurs as a result of the thought process and primary emotion.

SEEING OUR PAST IN LIGHT OF WHO WE ARE IN CHRIST

A. A New Creation in Christ
   When we accepted Christ, we were no longer a product of our past; we became a new creation in Christ (see 2 Corinthians 5:17). We have the awesome privilege of evaluating our past experiences in light of who we are today.

B. Forgiveness
   The second means by which we experience freedom from our past is through forgiveness. When we hold on to unforgiveness, it is we who are held captive.

WITNESS

1. If you are feeling angry, anxious or depressed, do you think it would be better not to be emotionally honest in the presence of non-Christians?

2. Would that be an effective or ineffective witness for Christ? Why?

DISCUSSION QUESTIONS

1. In what way could emotional dishonesty give the devil a foothold in your life?

2. What did you experience more in your home while growing up: emotional denial or indiscriminate expression? How has that affected your life?

3. In what ways can emotional dishonesty precipitate psychosomatic illnesses (i.e., physical illnesses whose root cause is emotional or mental in nature)?

4. How should you respond when someone who is hurting emotionally becomes verbally abusive?

5. How can you learn to recognize your emotional limitations?

6. What happens when something or someone triggers a strong emotion in you? What is your first reaction?

7. How can we become emotionally free from our past?

TAKING IT WITH YOU

SUGGESTIONS FOR QUIET TIME

Consider the emotional nature of the apostle Peter. First, look at some occasions when he acted impulsively or spoke too hastily:

- Matthew 16:21-23

- Matthew 17:1-5

- John 18:1-11

Now read Matthew 16:17-19 to see how Jesus looked beyond Peter's emotional outbursts to see Peter's potential, and finally, read Acts 2:14-41 to see how, under the power of the Holy Spirit, Peter fulfilled his potential and became the spokesperson of the Early Church.

THE BIG QUESTION

Before the next session, consider the following question:

How do you forgive from your heart those who have offended or deeply wounded you?

Note: For additional information on resolving specific emotional problems, we recommend the following resources:

- Neil T. Anderson and Rich Miller, *Getting Anger Under Control* (Eugene, OR: Harvest House, 2002) for information on resolving anger

- Neil T. Anderson and Rich Miller, *Freedom from Fear* (Eugene, OR: Harvest House, 1999) for information on resolving anxiety disorders

- Neil T. Anderson, *Overcoming Depression* (Ventura, CA: Regal Books, 2004) for information on resolving depression

---

FORGIVING FROM THE HEART

LET ALL BITTERNESS AND WRATH AND ANGER AND CLAMOR AND
SLANDER BE PUT AWAY FROM YOU, ALONG WITH ALL MALICE. BE KIND
TO ONE ANOTHER, TENDER-HEARTED, FORGIVING EACH OTHER, JUST AS
GOD IN CHRIST ALSO HAS FORGIVEN YOU.
EPHESIANS 4:31-32

WORD

Forgiveness is the central issue in Christianity, and forgiving from the heart is
the most important decision as Christians that we can make in order to experience our freedom in Christ. Most of us know that as Christians we should
forgive, but few of us fully understand what forgiveness is and how to forgive
others from the heart. Some of us are reluctant to forgive because to do so
would mean letting go of the desire to seek revenge; others of us hold on to
anger and unforgiveness with the false expectation that this will protect us in
the future. Forgiveness begins with God, and the love, mercy and grace that we
have received from God we are to extend to others.

OUR NEED TO EXTEND *AND* RECEIVE FORGIVENESS

A. Seeking the Forgiveness of Others (Matthew 5:23-24)
    If we have sinned against another person, we must not act as though we
    have done nothing wrong when the Holy Spirit is convicting us otherwise.
    We should go to that person with a repentant heart, seek his or her forgive-
    ness and offer to make reparations.

B. The Need to Forgive Others (Matthew 18:21-35)

- **Justice:** *Justice* is rightness or fairness; it is giving someone what he or she deserves. The consequence of sin is spiritual death, an eternity apart from God. And because we sin, that is also what we deserve.

- **Mercy:** Thankfully, God is merciful and sent Jesus to pay the price for our sins. God provided His own Son to pay for our sins with His very life. *Mercy* is not giving us what we deserve.

- **Grace:** Not only was God merciful to us in providing Jesus for our salvation, He also continually shows us *grace* by giving us that which we do not deserve.

WHAT FORGIVENESS IS *NOT*

A. It Is Not Forgetting
God doesn't forget our sins, but He has promised He will not take our past offenses and use them against us in the future.

B. It Is Not Tolerating Sin
Jesus forgives, but He doesn't tolerate sin, and neither should we.

C. It Is Not Denying Our Pain
Forgiveness is not stuffing our emotions or denying our pain. If we are going to forgive from our hearts, we have to do so from our hearts, which means acknowledging the hurt and the hate we feel.

WHAT FORGIVENESS IS (EPHESIANS 4:31-32)

A. It Is Agreeing to Live with the Consequences of Someone Else's Sin
Everybody is living with the consequences of somebody else's sin. We are all living with the consequences of Adam's sin. The only real choice is to live with the consequences of their sin in the bondage of bitterness or in the freedom of forgiveness.

B. It Is Letting God Be the Avenger (Romans 12:19-21)
God will mete out justice in His time, which is usually later than we would like it. Our responsibility is to be like Christ and live out the law of love.

C. It Is Bearing One Another's Burdens (Galatians 6:1-2)

When we are filled with the Holy Spirit, we will gently restore the offender. The burden we are asked to carry consists of the consequences of their sin.

The law of Christ, which it is our duty to fulfill, is the bearing of the cross. My brother's burden, which I must bear, is not only his outward lot, his natural characteristics and gifts, but quite literally his sin. And the only way to bear that sin is by forgiving it in the power of the cross of Christ in which I now share. Thus the call to follow Christ always means a call to share the work of forgiving men their sins. Forgiveness is the Christ-like suffering which it is the Christian's duty to bear. —Dietrich Bonhoeffer

---

HOW TO FORGIVE FROM THE HEART

A. The Healing Process

We forgive in order to heal. The healing process cannot start and reconciliation cannot take place until we face the crisis of forgiveness. In the Steps to Freedom in Christ, we encourage people to pray and ask God to reveal to their minds exactly whom they need to forgive.

B. The Temptation to Revisit Old Pain

If we have successfully forgiven someone, we should be able to think about the person or see him or her without being emotionally overcome. This doesn't mean that we will like him or her, but forgiveness allows us to go to the other person with purer motives—the love of Christ. To maintain our communion with God, our prayer should be the following:

Lord, I forgive [name] *for* [share every sin against you], *because it made me feel* [share how you felt about yourself, life and God as a result of that person's sin].

WITNESS

1. How might the issue of forgiveness challenge someone who is not yet a Christian?

2. How can you demonstrate forgiveness to someone who does not yet know the Lord?

DISCUSSION QUESTIONS

1. Do you agree that initially the crisis of forgiveness is between you and God rather than between you and the other person? Does it feel like that? Why?

2. Why is it important to make a distinction between seeking the forgiveness of others and forgiving others?

3. Define "justice," "mercy" and "grace" and illustrate how they should work out in our relationships with others.

4. What is the difference between forgiving and forgetting?

5. How can you forgive past abuse and set up scriptural boundaries to stop further abuse?

6. Who continues to feel pain when there is no forgiveness: the offender or the offended? Why?

7. How do we forgive from the heart?

8. What would you tell a person who refuses to forgive?

TAKING IT WITH YOU

SUGGESTION FOR QUIET TIME
Review this lesson and look up the pertinent passages that teach about forgiveness. Ask the Holy Spirit to bring to your mind those whom you need to forgive from your heart.

THE BIG QUESTION
Before the next session, consider the following question: How are we supposed to relate to others in terms of love, acceptance, judgment and discipline?

THE STEPS TO FREEDOM IN CHRIST

THE LORD'S BOND-SERVANT MUST NOT BE QUARRELSOME, BUT BE
KIND TO ALL, ABLE TO TEACH, PATIENT WHEN WRONGED, WITH GENTLENESS
CORRECTING THOSE WHO ARE IN OPPOSITION, IF PERHAPS GOD MAY GRANT
THEM REPENTANCE LEADING TO THE KNOWLEDGE OF THE TRUTH, AND THEY
MAY COME TO THEIR SENSES AND ESCAPE FROM THE SNARE OF THE DEVIL,
HAVING BEEN HELD CAPTIVE BY HIM TO DO HIS WILL.
2 TIMOTHY 2:24-26

THE WHOLE GOSPEL

God created Adam and Eve to be spiritually alive, which means that their souls were in union with God. Living in a dependent relationship with their heavenly Father, they were to exercise dominion over the earth. Acting independently of God, they chose to disobey Him and their choice to sin separated them from God. Consequently, all their descendants are born physically alive but spiritually dead—separated from God. Since we have all sinned and fallen short of the glory of God (see Romans 3:23), we remain separated from Him and cannot fulfill the original purpose for our creation, which is to glorify God and enjoy His presence forever. Satan became the rebel holder of authority and the god of this world. Jesus referred to him as the ruler of this world, and the apostle John wrote that the whole world lies in the power of the evil one (see 1 John 5:19).

Jesus came to undo the works of Satan (see 1 John 3:8) and to take upon Himself the sins of the world. By dying for our sins, Jesus removed the enmity that existed between God and those He created in His image. The resurrection of Christ brought new life to those who put their trust in Him. Every born-again believer's soul is again in union with God and that is most often communicated in the New Testament as being "in Christ," or "in Him." The apostle Paul explained that anyone who is *in Christ* is a new creation (see 2 Corinthians 5:17). The apostle John wrote, "But as many as received Him, to them He gave the right to become children of God, even to those who believe in His name" (John 1:12), and he also wrote, "See how great a love the Father has bestowed on us, that we would be called children of God; and such we are" (1 John 3:1).

No amount of effort on your part can save you and neither can any religious activity no matter how well intentioned. We are saved by faith and by faith alone. All that remains for us to do is put our trust in the finished work of Christ. "For by grace you have been saved through faith; and that not of yourselves, it is the gift of God; not as a result of works, so that no one may boast" (Ephesians 2:8-9). If you have never received Christ, you can do so right now. God knows the thoughts and intentions of your heart, so all you have to do is put your trust in God alone. You can express your decision in prayer as follows:

Dear Heavenly Father, thank You for sending Jesus to die on the cross for my sins. I acknowledge that I have sinned and that I cannot save myself. I believe that Jesus came to give me life, and by faith I now choose to receive You into my life as my Lord and Savior. By the power of Your indwelling presence enable me to be the person You created me to be. I pray that You would grant me repentance leading to a knowledge of the truth so that I can experience my freedom in Christ and be transformed by the renewing of my mind. In Jesus' precious name I pray. Amen.

ASSURANCE OF SALVATION

Paul wrote, "If you confess with your mouth Jesus as Lord, and believe in your heart that God raised Him from the dead, you will be saved" (Romans 10:9). Do you believe that God the Father raised Jesus from the dead? Did you invite Jesus to be your Lord and Savior? Then you are a child of God, and nothing can separate you from the love of Christ (see Romans 8:35). Your heavenly Father has sent His Holy Spirit to live within you and bear witness with your spirit that you are a child of God (see Romans 8:16). "You were sealed *in Him* with the Holy Spirit of promise" (Ephesians 1:13, emphasis added). The Holy Spirit will guide you into all truth (see John 16:13).

RESOLVING PERSONAL
AND SPIRITUAL CONFLICTS

Since we all were born spiritually dead in our trespasses and sin (see Ephesians 2:1), we had neither the presence of God in our lives nor the knowledge of His ways. Consequently, we all learned to live our lives independently of God. When we became new creations in Christ, our minds were not instantly renewed. That is why Paul wrote, "Do not be conformed any longer to this world, but be transformed by the renewing of your mind" (Romans 12:2).

Then you will be able to test and approve what God's will is—His good, pleasing, and perfect will (see Romans 12:2). That is why new Christians struggle with many of the same old thoughts and habits. Their minds have been previously programmed to live independently of God, and that is the chief characteristic of our old nature or flesh. As new creations in Christ, we have the mind of Christ, and the Holy Spirit will lead us into all truth. To experience our freedom in Christ and to grow in the grace of God require repentance, which literally means a change of mind. Repentance is not something we can do on our own; therefore, we need to submit to God and resist the devil (see James 4:7). The Steps to Freedom in Christ (the Steps) are designed to help you do that. Submitting to God is the critical issue. He is the wonderful counselor and the One who grants repentance leading to a knowledge of the truth (see 2 Timothy 2:24-26).

The Steps cover seven critical issues between ourselves and God. We will not experience our freedom in Christ if we seek false guidance, believe lies, fail to forgive others as we have been forgiven, live in rebellion, respond in pride, fail to acknowledge our sin and continue in the sins of our ancestors. "He who conceals his transgressions will not prosper, but he who confesses and forsakes [renounces] them will find compassion" (Proverbs 28:13). "Therefore since we have this ministry, as we received mercy, we do not lose heart, but we have renounced things hidden because of shame, not walking in craftiness or adulterating the word of God, but by the manifestation of truth" (2 Corinthians 4:1-2).

Even though Satan is defeated, he still rules this world through a hierarchy of demons who tempt, accuse and deceive those who fail to put on the armor of God, stand firm in their faith and take every thought captive to the obedience of Christ. Our sanctuary is our identity and position in Christ, and we have all the protection we need to live victorious lives; but if we fail to assume our responsibility and give ground to Satan, we will suffer the consequences of our sinful attitudes and actions. The good news is, we can repent and reclaim all that we have in Christ, and that is what the Steps will enable you to do.

PROCESSING THE STEPS

Ideally, it would be best if you read *Victory Over the Darkness* and *The Bondage Breaker* before you process the Steps.[1] Audio books and audiocassettes are also available from Freedom in Christ Ministries. The best way to go through the Steps is to process them with a trained encourager. The book *Discipleship Counseling* explains the theology and process.[2]

You can also go through the Steps on your own. Every step is explained so you will have no trouble doing that. I suggest you find a quiet place where you can process the Steps out loud. If you experience some mental interference, just ignore it and continue on. Thoughts such as *This isn't going to work* or *I don't believe this*, or blasphemous, condemning and accusing thoughts have no power over you unless you believe them. They are just thoughts and it doesn't make any difference if they originate from yourself, an external source or from Satan and his demons. Such thoughts will be resolved when you have fully repented.

If you are working with a trained encourager, share any mental or physical opposition that you are experiencing. The mind is the control center, and you will not lose control in the freedom appointment if you don't lose control of your mind. The best way to do that, if you are being mentally harassed, is to just share it. Exposing the lies to the light breaks the power of the darkness.

Remember, you are a child of God and seated with Christ in the heavenlies. That means you have the authority and power to do His will. The Steps don't set you free. Jesus sets you free, and you will progressively experience that freedom as you respond to Him in faith and repentance.

Don't worry about any demonic interference; most do not experience any. It doesn't make any difference if Satan has a little role or a bigger role; the critical issue is your relationship with God and that is what you are resolving. This is a ministry of reconciliation. Once those issues are resolved, Satan has no right to remain. Successfully completing this repentance process is not an end; but rather, it is the beginning of growth. Unless these issues are resolved, however, the growth process will be stalled and your Christian life will be stagnant.

PREPARATION

Processing the Steps can play a major role in your continuing process of discipleship. The purpose is to get you firmly rooted in Christ. It doesn't take long to establish your identity and freedom in Christ, but there is no such thing as instant maturity. Renewing your mind and conforming to the image of God is a lifelong process. May the Lord grace you with His presence as you seek to do His will. Once you have experienced your freedom in Christ, you can help others experience the joy of their salvation. Begin the Steps with the following prayer and declaration:

Prayer: *Dear Heavenly Father, You are present in this room and in my life. You alone are all-knowing, all-powerful and everywhere present, and I worship You alone. I declare my dependency on You, for apart from You I can do nothing. I choose to believe Your Word which teaches that all authority in heaven and on*

Earth belongs to the resurrected Christ, and being alive in Christ I have the author-ity to resist the devil as I submit to You. I ask that You fill me with Your Holy Spirit and guide me into all truth. I ask for Your complete protection and guidance as I seek to know You and do Your will. In the wonderful name of Jesus, I pray. Amen.

Declaration: *In the name and authority of the Lord Jesus Christ, I command Satan and all evil spirits to release their hold on me in order that I can be free to know and choose to do the will of God. As a child of God who is seated with Christ in the heavenly places, I declare that every enemy of the Lord Jesus Christ in my presence be bound. Satan and all his demons cannot inflict any pain or in any way prevent God's will from being done in my life today because I belong to the Lord Jesus Christ.*

REVIEW OF YOUR LIFE

Before going through the Steps, review the following events of your life to dis-cern specific areas that need to be addressed:

FAMILY HISTORY

- Religious history of parents and grandparents
- Home life from childhood through high school
- History of physical or emotional illness in the family
- Adoption, foster care, guardians

PERSONAL HISTORY

- Eating habits (bulimia, anorexia, compulsive eating)
- Addictions (cigarettes, drugs, alcohol)
- Prescription medications (what for?)
- Sleeping patterns, dreams and nightmares
- Rape or any other sexual, physical or emotional abuse
- Thought life (obsessive, blasphemous, condemning and distracting thoughts; poor concentration; fantasy; suicidal thoughts; fearful; jeal-ous; confused; guilt and shame)
- Mental interference during church, prayer or Bible study
- Emotional life (anger, anxiety, depression, bitterness and fear)
- Spiritual journey (salvation: when, how and assurance)

Notes
1. Neil T. Anderson, *Victory Over the Darkness* (Ventura, CA: Regal Books, 2000); Neil T. Anderson, *The Bondage Breaker* (Eugene, OR: Harvest House, 2000).
2. Neil T. Anderson, *Discipleship Counseling* (Ventura, CA: Regal Books, 2003).

STEP 1

COUNTERFEIT VERSUS REAL

The first step toward experiencing your freedom in Christ is to renounce (verbally reject) all involvement (past or present) with occult, cult or false religious teachings or practices. Participation in any group that denies that Jesus Christ is Lord and/or elevates any teaching or book to the level of (or above) the Bible must be renounced.

In addition, groups that require dark, secret initiations, ceremonies, vows, pacts or covenants need to be renounced. God does not take lightly false guidance. "As for the person who turns to mediums and to spiritists . . . I will also set My face against that person and will cut him off from among his people" (Leviticus 20:6). Since you don't want the Lord to cut you off, ask Him to guide you as follows:

> *Dear Heavenly Father, please bring to my mind anything and everything that I have done knowingly or unknowingly that involves occult, cult, false religious teachings or practices. I want to experience Your freedom by renouncing any and all false guidance. In Jesus' name I pray. Amen.*

The Lord may bring things to your mind that you had forgotten, even things you participated in as a game or thought were jokes. You might even have been passively yet curiously watching others participate in counterfeit religious practices. The purpose is to renounce all counterfeit spiritual experiences and their beliefs.

To help bring these things to your mind, prayerfully consider the following Non-Christian Spiritual Checklist on the next page. Then pray the prayer following the checklist to renounce each activity or group the Lord brings to mind. He may reveal to you ones that are not on the list. Be especially aware of your need to renounce non-Christian folk religious practices if you have grown up in another culture. It is important that you prayerfully renounce them **out loud.**

Non-Christian Spiritual Checklist

(Check all in which you have participated.)

- ❑ Out-of-body experience
- ❑ Ouija board
- ❑ Bloody Mary
- ❑ Occult games
- ❑ Magic Eight Ball
- ❑ Spells or curses
- ❑ Mental telepathy/control
- ❑ Automatic writing
- ❑ Trances
- ❑ Spirit guides
- ❑ Fortune-telling/divination
- ❑ Tarot cards
- ❑ Levitation
- ❑ Witchcraft/wicca/sorcery
- ❑ Satanism
- ❑ Palm reading
- ❑ Astrology/horoscopes
- ❑ Hypnosis
- ❑ Astral projection
- ❑ Seances/mediums/channelers
- ❑ Black or white magic
- ❑ Blood pacts
- ❑ Fetishism/crystals/charms
- ❑ Sexual spirits
- ❑ Martial arts (mysticism)
- ❑ Superstitions
- ❑ Mormonism (Latter-day Saints)

- ❑ Jehovah's Witness
- ❑ New Age (teachings, medicine)
- ❑ Masons
- ❑ Christian Science/Mind Science
- ❑ Unification Church (Moonies)
- ❑ The Forum (EST)
- ❑ Church of Scientology
- ❑ Unitarianism/Universalism
- ❑ Silva Mind Control
- ❑ Transcendental Meditation (TM)
- ❑ Yoga (religion, not the exercise)
- ❑ Hare Krishna
- ❑ Bahaism
- ❑ Native American spirit worship
- ❑ Islam
- ❑ Hinduism
- ❑ Buddhism (including Zen)
- ❑ Black Muslim
- ❑ Rosicrucianism
- ❑ False gods (money, sex, power, pleasure, certain people)
- ❑ Other (such as non-Christian religions; cults; movies; music; books; video games; comics or fantasy games that glorify Satan, which precipitated nightmares or mental battles; all other questionable spiritual experiences including spiritual visitations and nightmares)

Additional Questions to Help You Become Aware of
Counterfeit Religious Experiences

1. Do you now have, or have you ever had, an imaginary friend, spirit guide or
   angel offering you guidance or companionship? (If it has a name, renounce
   it by name.)

2. Have you ever heard voices in your head or had repeating, nagging thoughts
   (such as *I'm dumb, I'm ugly, Nobody loves me* or *I can't do anything right*) as if there
   were a conversation going on inside your head?

3. Have you ever been hypnotized, attended a New Age seminar or consulted a
   medium or spiritist?

4. Have you ever made a secret vow or pact (or inner vow; i.e., *I will never* . . .)?

5. Have you ever been involved in a satanic ritual or attended a concert or event
   in which Satan was the focus?

Once you have completed your checklist and the questions, confess and renounce every false religious practice, belief, ceremony, vow or pact in which you
were involved by praying the following prayer **aloud**:

> *Lord Jesus, I confess that I have participated in* [specifically name every belief
> and involvement related to all that you have checked above], *and I re-
> nounce them all as counterfeits. I pray that You will fill me with Your Holy Spirit
> so that I may be guided by You. Thank You that in Christ I am forgiven. Amen.*

SATANIC WORSHIP

People who have been subjected to Satanic Ritual Abuse (SRA) need the help of
someone who understands dissociative disorders and spiritual warfare. If you
have been involved in any form of satanic worship, say **aloud** the Special Renun-
ciations on the following page.

Read across the page, renouncing the first item in the column entitled
"Kingdom of Darkness," and then announcing the truth in the column entitled "Kingdom of Light." Continue down the page in this manner. Notice that
satanic worship is the antithesis of true worship.

Kingdom of Darkness	Kingdom of Light
I renounce ever signing my name over to Satan or having my name signed over to Satan.	I announce that my name is now written in the Lamb's book of life.
I renounce any ceremony in which I have been wed to Satan.	I announce that I am the bride of Christ.
I renounce any and all covenants that I made with Satan.	I announce that I am under the new covenant with Christ.
I renounce all satanic assignments for my life, including duties, marriage and children.	I announce and commit myself to know and do only the will of God and accept only His guidance.
I renounce all spirit guides assigned to me.	I accept only the leading of the Holy Spirit.
I renounce ever giving my blood in the service of Satan.	I trust only the blood of the Lord Jesus Christ.
I renounce ever eating flesh or drinking blood for satanic worship.	By faith I symbolically eat only the flesh and drink only the blood of Jesus in Holy Communion.
I renounce any and all guardians and satanist parents who were assigned to me.	I announce that God is my Father and the Holy Spirit is my guardian by whom I am sealed.
I renounce any baptism whereby I have been identified with Satan.	I announce that I have been baptized into Christ Jesus.
I renounce any and all sacrifices that were made on my behalf by which Satan may claim ownership of me.	I announce that only the sacrifice of Christ has any hold on me. I belong to Him. I have been purchased by the blood of the Lamb.

STEP 2

DECEPTION VERSUS TRUTH

The Christian life is lived by faith according to what God says is true. Jesus is the truth, the Holy Spirit is the Spirit of truth, God's Word is truth, and we are to speak the truth in love (see John 14:6; 16:13; 17:17; Ephesians 4:15). The biblical response to truth is *faith*, regardless of whether we *feel* it is true. In addition, Christians are to have no part in lying, deceiving, stretching the truth, or anything else associated with falsehood. Lies keep us in bondage, but it is the truth that sets us free (see John 8:32). David wrote, "How blessed [happy] is the man . . . in whose spirit there is no deceit" (Psalm 32:2). Joy and freedom come from walking in the truth.

We find the strength to walk in the light of honesty and transparency before God and others (see 1 John 1:7) when we know that God loves and accepts us just as we are. We can face reality, acknowledge our sins and not try to hide. Begin this commitment to truth by praying the following prayer **aloud**. Don't let any opposing thoughts, such as *This is a waste of time* or *I wish I could believe this, but I can't*, keep you from pressing forward. God will strengthen you as you rely on Him.

Dear Heavenly Father, You are the truth and I desire to live by faith according to Your truth. The truth will set me free, but in many ways I have been deceived by the father of lies and the philosophies of this fallen world, and I have deceived myself. I choose to walk in the light, knowing that You love and accept me just as I am. As I consider areas of possible deception, I invite the Spirit of truth to guide me into all truth. Please protect me from all deception as You "search me, O God, and know my heart; try me and know my anxious thoughts; and see if there be any hurtful way in me, and lead me in the everlasting way" [Psalm 139:23-24]. In the name of Jesus, I pray. Amen.

Next, prayerfully consider the lists in the following three exercises, using the prayer at the end of each exercise in order to confess any ways you have given in to deception or wrongly defended yourself. Of course, you cannot instantly renew your mind, but the process will never begin unless you first acknowledge your mental strongholds or defense mechanisms, which are sometimes called flesh patterns.

Ways You Can Be Deceived by the World

❑ Believing that acquiring money and things will bring lasting happiness (see Matthew 13:22; 1 Timothy 6:10)

❑ Believing that excessive food and alcohol can relieve your stress and make you happy (see Proverbs 23:19-21)

❑ Believing that an attractive body and personality will get you what you need (see Proverbs 31:30; 1 Peter 3:3-4)

❑ Believing that gratifying sexual lust will bring lasting satisfaction (see Ephesians 4:22; 1 Peter 2:11)

❑ Believing that you can sin and get away without any negative consequences (see Hebrews 3:12-13)

❑ Believing you need more than what God has given you in Christ (see 2 Corinthians 11:2-4,13-15)

❑ Believing that you can do whatever you want and no one can touch you (see Proverbs 16:18; Obadiah 3; 1 Peter 5:5)

❑ Believing that unrighteous people who refuse to accept Christ go to heaven anyway (see 1 Corinthians 6:9-11)

❑ Believing that you can associate with bad company and not become corrupted (see 1 Corinthians 15:33-34)

❑ Believing that you can read, see or listen to anything and not be corrupted (see Proverbs 4:23-27; Matthew 5:28)

❑ Believing that there are no consequences on Earth for your sin (see Galatians 6:7-8)

❑ Believing you must gain the approval of certain people in order to be happy (see Galatians 1:10)

❑ Believing you must measure up to certain standards in order to feel good about yourself (see Galatians 3:2-3; 5:1)

Lord Jesus, I confess that I have been deceived by [confess the items you checked above]. *I thank You for Your forgiveness, and I commit myself to believe only Your truth. In Jesus' name I pray. Amen.*

WAYS YOU DECEIVE YOURSELF

❑ Hearing God's Word but not doing what it says (see James 1:22)

❑ Saying you have no sin (see 1 John 1:8)

❑ Thinking you are something you are really not (see Galatians 6:3)

❑ Thinking you are wise in this worldly age (see 1 Corinthians 3:18-19)

❑ Thinking you can be truly religious but not bridle your tongue (see James 1:26)

❑ Thinking that God is the source of your problems (see Lamentations 3)

❑ Thinking you can live your life without the help of anyone else (see 1 Corinthians 12:14-20)

Lord Jesus, I confess that I have deceived myself by [confess the items checked above]. *Thank You for Your forgiveness. I commit myself to believe only Your truth. In Jesus' name I pray. Amen.*

WAYS YOU WRONGLY DEFEND YOURSELF

❑ Denial of reality (conscious or unconscious)

❑ Fantasy (escaping reality through daydreaming, TV, movies, music, computer or video games, drugs, alcohol)

❑ Emotional insulation (withdrawing from people or keeping people at a distance to avoid rejection)

❑ Regression (reverting to less threatening times)

❑ Displaced anger (taking out frustrations on innocent people)

❑ Projection (attributing to another what you find unacceptable in yourself)

❑ Rationalization (making excuses for your own poor behavior)

❑ Lying (protecting yourself through falsehoods)

❑ Blaming yourself (when you are not responsible) and others

❑ Hypocrisy (presenting a false image)

Lord Jesus, I confess that I have wrongly defended myself by [confess the items checked above]. *Thank You for Your forgiveness. I trust You to defend and protect me. In Jesus' name I pray. Amen.*

The wrong ways we have employed to shield ourselves from pain and rejection are often deeply ingrained in our lives. You may need additional discipling or counseling to learn how to allow Christ to be your rock, fortress, deliverer and refuge (see Psalm 18:1-2). The more you learn how loving, powerful and protective God is, the more you'll be likely to trust Him. The more you realize His complete acceptance of you in Christ, the more you'll be released to be open, honest and (in a healthy way) vulnerable before God and others.

The New Age movement has twisted the concept of faith by teaching that we make something true by believing it. That is false. We cannot create reality with our minds; only God can do that. Our responsibility is to *face* reality and choose to believe what God says is true. True biblical faith is choosing to believe and act upon what is true, because God has said it is true, and He is the Truth. Faith is something you decide to do, not something you feel like doing. Believing something doesn't make it true; *it's already true, therefore we choose to believe it!*

Everybody lives by faith. The only difference between Christian faith and non-Christian faith is the object of our faith. If the object of our faith is not trustworthy, then no amount of believing will change that. That's why our faith must be grounded on the solid rock of God's perfect, unchanging character and the truth of His Word. For two thousand years Christians have known the importance of verbally and publicly declaring truth.

Read **aloud** the following Statements of Truth, and carefully consider what you are professing. You may find it helpful to read them **aloud** daily for several weeks, which will help renew your mind to the truth.

STATEMENTS OF TRUTH

1. I recognize that there is only one true and living God who exists as the Father, Son and Holy Spirit. He is worthy of all honor, praise and glory as the One who made all things and holds all things together. [See Exodus 20:2-3; Colossians 1:16-17.]

2. I recognize Jesus Christ as the Messiah, the Word who became flesh and dwelt among us. I believe that He came to destroy the works of the devil and that He disarmed the rulers and authorities and made a public display of them, having triumphed over them. [See John 1:1,14; Colossians 2:15; 1 John 3:8.]

3. I believe that God demonstrated His own love for me in that while I was still a sinner, Christ died for me. I believe that He has delivered me from the do-main of darkness and transferred me to His kingdom, and in Him I have redemption, the forgiveness of sins. [See Romans 5:8; Colossians 1:13-14.]

4. I believe that I am now a child of God and that I am seated with Christ in the heavenlies. I believe that I was saved by the grace of God through faith and that it was a gift and not a result of any works on my part. [See Ephesians 2:6,8-9; 1 John 3:1-3.]

5. I choose to be strong in the Lord and in the strength of His might. I put no confidence in the flesh, for the weapons of warfare are not of the flesh but are divinely powerful for the destruction of strongholds. I put on the full armor of God. I resolve to stand firm in my faith and resist the evil one. [See 2 Corinthians 10:4; Ephesians 6:10-20; Philippians 3:3.]

6. I believe that apart from Christ I can do nothing, so I declare my complete dependence on Him. I choose to abide in Christ in order to bear much fruit and glorify my Father. I announce to Satan that Jesus is my Lord. I reject any and all counterfeit gifts or works of Satan in my life. [See John 15:5,8; 1 Corinthians 12:3.]

7. I believe that the truth will set me free and that Jesus is the truth. If He sets me free, I will be free indeed. I recognize that walking in the light is the only path of true fellowship with God and man. Therefore, I stand against all of Satan's deception by taking every thought captive in obedience to Christ.

I declare that the Bible is the only authoritative standard for truth and life. [See John 8:32,36; 14:6; 2 Corinthians 10:5; 2 Timothy 3:15-17; 1 John 1:3-7.]

8. I choose to present my body to God as a living and holy sacrifice and the members of my body as instruments of righteousness. I choose to renew my mind by the living Word of God in order that I may prove that the will of God is good, acceptable and perfect. I put off the old self with its evil practices and I put on the new self. I declare myself to be a new creation in Christ. [See Romans 6:13; 12:1-2; 2 Corinthians 5:17; Colossians 3:9-10.]

9. By faith, I choose to be filled with the Spirit so that I can be guided into all truth. I choose to walk by the Spirit so that I will not carry out the desires of the flesh. [See John 16:13; Galatians 5:16; Ephesians 5:18.]

10. I renounce all selfish goals and choose the ultimate goal of love. I choose to obey the two greatest commandments: to love the Lord my God with all my heart, soul, mind and strength and to love my neighbor as myself. [See Matthew 22:37-39; 1 Timothy 1:5.]

11. I believe the Lord Jesus has all authority in heaven and on Earth and is the head over all rule and authority. I am complete in Him. I believe that Satan and his demons are subject to me in Christ since I am a member of Christ's Body. Therefore, I obey the command to submit to God and resist the devil, and I command Satan in the name of Jesus Christ to leave my presence. [See Matthew 28:18; Ephesians 1:19-23; Colossians 2:10; James 4:7.]

STEP 3

BITTERNESS VERSUS FORGIVENESS

We are called to be merciful just as our heavenly Father is merciful (see Luke 6:36) and forgive others as we have been forgiven (see Ephesians 4:31-32). Doing so sets us free from our past and doesn't allow Satan to take advantage of us (see 2 Corinthians 2:10-11). Ask God to bring to your mind the people you need to forgive by praying the following prayer **aloud**:

> *Dear Heavenly Father, I thank You for the riches of Your kindness, forbearance and patience toward me, knowing that Your kindness has led me to repentance. I confess that I have not shown that same kindness and patience toward those who have hurt or offended me [see Romans 2:4]. Instead, I have held on to my anger, bitterness and resentment toward them. Please bring to my mind all the people I need to forgive in order that I may now do so. In Jesus' name I pray. Amen.*

On a separate sheet of paper, list the names of people who come to your mind. At this point don't question whether you need to forgive them. Often we hold things against ourselves as well, punishing ourselves for wrong choices we've made in the past. Write "myself" at the bottom of your list if you need to forgive yourself. Forgiving yourself is accepting the truth that God has already forgiven you in Christ. If God forgives you, you can forgive yourself!

Also write down "Thoughts Against God" at the bottom of your list. Obviously, God has never done anything wrong, so He doesn't need our forgiveness; but we need to let go of our disappointments with our heavenly Father. People often harbor angry thoughts against Him because He did not do what they wanted Him to do. Those feelings of anger or resentment toward God need to be released.

Before you begin working through the process of forgiving those on your list, review what forgiveness is and what it is not. The critical points are highlighted in bold print.

- **Forgiveness is not forgetting.** People who want to forget all that was done to them will find they cannot do it. When God says that He will "not remember your sins" (Isaiah 43:25), He is saying that He will not use the past against us. Forgetting is a long-term by-product of forgiveness, but it is never a means toward it. Don't put off forgiving those who have hurt you, hoping the pain will go away. Once you choose to forgive someone, *then* Christ will heal your wounds. We don't heal in order to forgive; we forgive in order to heal.

- **Forgiveness is a choice, a decision of the will.** Since God requires you to forgive, it is something you can do. Some people hold on to their anger as a means of protecting themselves against further abuse, but all they are doing is hurting themselves. Others want revenge. The Bible teaches, " 'Vengeance is mine, I will repay,' says the Lord" (Romans 12:19). Let God deal with the person. Let him or her off your hook because as long as you refuse to forgive someone, you are still hooked to that person. You are still chained to your past, bound up in your bitterness. By forgiving, you let the other person off your hook, but he or she is not off God's hook. You must trust that God will deal with the person justly and fairly, something you simply cannot do.

  But you don't know how much this person hurt me! No other human really knows another person's pain, but Jesus does, and He instructed us to forgive others for our sake. Until you let go of your bitterness and hatred, the person is still hurting you. Nobody can fix your past, but you can be free from it. What you gain by forgiving is freedom from your past and those who have abused you. To forgive is to set a captive free and then realize you were the captive.

- **Forgiveness is agreeing to live with the consequences of another person's sin.** We are all living with the consequences of someone else's sin. The only choice is whether to do so in the *bondage of bitterness* or in the *freedom of forgiveness*. But where is the justice? The Cross makes forgiveness legally and morally right. Jesus died, once for all our sins. We are to forgive as Christ has forgiven us. He did that by taking upon Himself the consequences of our sins. God "made Him who knew no sin to be sin on our behalf, so that we might become the righteousness of God in Him" (2 Corinthians 5:21). Do not wait for the other person to ask for your forgiveness. Remember, Jesus did not wait for those who were crucifying Him to apologize before He forgave them. Even while they mocked and jeered at Him, He prayed, "Father, forgive them; for they do not know what they are doing" (Luke 23:34).

- **Forgive from your heart.** Allow God to bring to the surface the painful memories and acknowledge how you feel toward those who've hurt you. If your forgiveness doesn't touch the emotional core of your life, it will be incomplete. Too often we're afraid of the pain, so we bury our emotions deep down inside us. Let God bring them to the surface, so He can begin to heal those damaged emotions.

- **Forgiveness is choosing not to hold someone's sin against him or her anymore.** It is common for bitter people to bring up past offenses with those who have hurt them. They want them to feel as bad as they do! But we must let go of the past and choose to reject any thought of revenge. This doesn't mean you continue to put up with the abuse. God does not tolerate sin and neither should you. You will need to set up scriptural boundaries that put a stop to further abuse. Take a stand against sin while continuing to exercise grace and forgiveness toward those who hurt you. If you need help setting scriptural boundaries to protect yourself from further abuse, talk to a trusted friend, counselor or pastor.

- **Don't wait until you feel like forgiving.** You will never get there. Make the hard choice to forgive, even if you don't feel like it. Once you choose to forgive, Satan will lose his hold on you, and God will heal your damaged emotions.

Start with the first person on your list, and make the choice to forgive him or her for every painful memory that comes to your mind. Stay with that individual until you are sure you have dealt with all the remembered pain. Then work your way down the list in the same way.

As you begin forgiving people, God may bring to your mind painful memories that you've totally forgotten. Let Him do this, even if it hurts. God is surfacing those painful memories so that you can face them once for all time and let them go. Don't excuse the offender's behavior, even if it is someone you are really close to.

Don't say, "Lord, please help me to forgive." He is already helping you and will be with you all the way through the process. Don't say, "Lord, I want to forgive," because that bypasses the hard choice we have to make. Say, "Lord, I choose to forgive these people and what they did to me." For every painful memory that God reveals for each person on your list, pray **aloud**:

Lord Jesus, I choose to forgive [name the person] *for* [what they did or failed to do] *because it made me feel* [share the painful feelings; i.e., rejected, dirty, worthless, inferior, etc.].

After you have forgiven every person for every painful memory, then pray the following prayer:

Lord Jesus, I choose not to hold on to my resentment. I relinquish my right to seek revenge and ask You to heal my damaged emotions. Thank You for setting me free from the bondage of my bitterness. I now ask You to bless those who have hurt me. In Jesus' name I pray. Amen.

Before we came to Christ, thoughts were raised up in our minds against a true knowledge of God (see 2 Corinthians 10:3-5). Even as believers we have harbored resentments toward God and that will hinder our walk with Him. We should have a healthy fear of God—awe of His holiness, power and presence— but we fear no punishment from Him. Romans 8:15 reads, "For you have not received a spirit of slavery leading to fear again, but you have received a spirit of adoption as sons by which we cry out, 'Abba! Father!'"

The following exercise will help renew your mind to a true knowledge of your heavenly Father. Read the list aloud starting with the left column and then reading the corresponding right column. Begin each one with the statement in bold at the top of that list.

ACKNOWLEDGING THE TRUTH ABOUT YOUR FATHER GOD

I renounce the lie that my Father God is	I choose to believe the truth that my Father God is
Distant and disinterested	Intimate and involved [see Psalm 39:1-18]
Insensitive and uncaring	Kind and compassionate [see Psalm 103:8-14]
Stern and demanding	Accepting and filled with joy and love [see Zephaniah 3:17; Romans 15:7]
Passive and cold	Warm and affectionate [see Isaiah 40:11; Hosea 11:3-4]
Absent or too busy for me	Always with me and eager to be with me [see Jeremiah 31:20; Ezekiel 34:11-16; Hebrews 13:5]
Impatient, angry and rejecting	Patient and slow to anger [see Exodus 34:6; 2 Peter 3:9]
Mean, cruel or abusive	Loving, gentle and protective [see Jeremiah 31:3; Isaiah 42:3; Psalm 18:2]
Trying to take all the fun out of life	Trustworthy and wants to give me a full life; His will is good, perfect and acceptable for me [see Lamentations 3:22-23; John 10:10; Romans 12:1-2]
Controlling or manipulative	Full of grace and mercy, and He gives me freedom to fail [see Luke 15:11-16; Hebrews 4:15-16]
Condemning or unforgiving	Tenderhearted and forgiving; His heart and arms are always open to me [see Psalm 130:1-4; Luke 15:17-24]
A nit-picking, demanding perfectionist	Committed to my growth and proud of me as His beloved child [see Romans 8:28-29; Hebrews 12:5-11; 2 Corinthians 7:4]

I AM THE APPLE OF HIS EYE!
(SEE DEUTERONOMY 32:9-10.)

STEP 4

REBELLION VERSUS SUBMISSION

We live in rebellious times. Many people sit in judgment of those in authority over them, and they submit only when it is convenient, or they do so in the fear of being caught. The Bible instructs us to pray for those in authority over us (see 1 Timothy 2:1-2) and to submit to governing authorities (see Romans 13:1-7). Rebelling against God and His established authority leaves us spiritually vulnerable. The only time God permits us to disobey earthly leaders is when they require us to do something morally wrong or attempt to rule outside the realm of their authority. To have a submissive spirit and servant's heart, pray the following prayer **aloud**:

> *Dear Heavenly Father, You have said that rebellion is as the sin of witchcraft and insubordination is as iniquity and idolatry* [see 1 Samuel 15:23]. *I know that I have not always been submissive but instead have rebelled in my heart against You and against those You have placed in authority over me in attitude and in action. Please show me all the ways I have been rebellious. I choose now to adopt a submissive spirit and a servant's heart. In Jesus' name I pray. Amen.*

It is an act of faith to trust God to work in our lives through something less than perfect leaders, but that is what God is asking us to do. Should those in positions of leadership or power abuse their authority and break the laws that are designed to protect innocent people, you need to seek help from a higher authority. Many states require certain types of abuse to be reported to a governmental agency. If that is your situation, we urge you to get the help you need immediately. Don't, however, assume that someone in authority is violating God's Word just because he or she is telling you to do something you don't like. God has set up specific lines of authority to protect us and give order to society. It is the position of authority that we respect. Without governing authorities, every society would be chaos. From the list below, allow the Lord to show you any specific ways you have been rebellious and use the prayer that follows to confess those sins He brings to mind.

❑ Civil government, including traffic laws, tax laws and your attitude toward government officials (see Romans 13:1-7; 1 Timothy 2:1-4; 1 Peter 2:13-17)

❑ Parents, stepparents or legal guardians (see Ephesians 6:1-3)

❑ Teachers, coaches and school officials (see Romans 13:1-4)

❑ Employers—past and present (see 1 Peter 2:18-23)

❑ Husband (see 1 Peter 3:1-4) or wife (see Ephesians 5:21; 1 Peter 3:7)
(**Note to Husbands:** Ask the Lord if your lack of love for your wife
could be fostering a rebellious spirit within her. If so, confess that as
a violation of Ephesians 5:22-33.)

❑ Church leaders (see Hebrews 13:7)

❑ God (see Daniel 9:5,9)

For each way in which the Spirit of God brings to your mind that you have
been rebellious, use the following prayer to specifically confess that sin:

Lord Jesus, I confess that I have been rebellious toward [name or position] *by*
[specifically confess what you did or did not do]. *Thank You for Your forgiveness. I choose to be submissive and obedient to Your Word. In Jesus' name
I pray. Amen.*

STEP 5

PRIDE VERSUS HUMILITY

Pride comes before a fall, but God gives grace to the humble (see James 4:6; 1 Peter 5:1-10). Humility is confidence properly placed in God, and we are instructed to "put no confidence in the flesh" (Philippians 3:3). We are to be "strong in the Lord and in the strength of His might" (Ephesians 6:10). Proverbs 3:5-7 urges us to trust in the Lord with all our hearts and to not lean on our own understanding. Use the following prayer to ask for God's guidance concerning ways that you may be prideful:

> *Dear Heavenly Father, You have said that pride goes before destruction and an arrogant spirit before stumbling. I confess that I have focused on my own needs and desires and not others'. I have not always denied myself, picked up my cross daily and followed You. I have relied on my own strength and resources instead of resting in Yours. I have placed my will before Yours and centered my life around myself instead of You. I confess my pride and selfishness and pray that all ground gained in my life by the enemies of the Lord Jesus Christ would be canceled. I choose to rely upon the Holy Spirit's power and guidance so that I will do nothing from selfishness or empty conceit. But with humility of mind, I choose to regard others as more important than myself. I acknowledge You as my Lord, and confess that apart from You I can do nothing of lasting significance. Please examine my heart and show me the specific ways I have lived my life in pride. In the gentle and humble name of Jesus, I pray. Amen. [See Proverbs 16:18; Matthew 6:33; 16:24; Romans 12:10; Philippians 2:3.]*

Pray through the list below and use the prayer following to confess any sins of pride the Lord brings to mind:

❑ Having a stronger desire to do my will than God's will

❑ Leaning too much on my own understanding and experience rather than seeking God's guidance through prayer and His Word

❑ Relying on my own strengths and resources instead of depending on the power of the Holy Spirit

❑ Being more concerned about controlling others than in developing self-control

- ❏ Being too busy doing seemingly important and selfish things rather than seeking and doing God's will

- ❏ Having a tendency to think that I have no needs

- ❏ Finding it hard to admit when I am wrong

- ❏ Being more concerned about pleasing people than pleasing God

- ❏ Being overly concerned about getting the credit I feel I deserve

- ❏ Thinking I am more humble, spiritual, religious or devoted than others

- ❏ Being driven to obtain recognition through attaining degrees, titles and positions

- ❏ Often feeling that my needs are more important than another person's needs

- ❏ Considering myself better than others because of my academic, artistic or athletic abilities and accomplishments

- ❏ Having feelings of inferiority appearing as false humility

- ❏ Not waiting on God

- ❏ Other ways I have thought more highly of myself than I should

For each of the above areas that has been true in your life, pray **aloud**:

Lord Jesus, I agree I have been proud by [name each item you checked above]. *Thank You for Your forgiveness. I choose to humble myself before You and others. I choose to place all my confidence in You and not to put confidence in my flesh. In Jesus' name I pray. Amen.*

STEP 6

BONDAGE VERSUS FREEDOM

Many times we feel trapped in a vicious cycle of sin-confess-sin-confess that never seems to end. We can become very discouraged and end up just giving up and giving in to the sins of the flesh. In order to experience our freedom, we must follow James 4:7: "Submit therefore to God. Resist the devil and he will flee from you." We submit to God by confession of sin and repentance (turning away from sin). We resist the devil by rejecting his lies. We must walk in the truth and put on the full armor of God (see Ephesians 6:10-20).

Sin that has become a habit often may require help from a trusted brother or sister in Christ. James 5:16 says, "Confess your sins to one another, and pray for one another so that you may be healed. The effective prayer of a righteous man can accomplish much." Sometimes the assurance of 1 John 1:9 is enough: "If we confess our sins, He is faithful and righteous to forgive us our sins and to cleanse us from all unrighteousness."

Remember, confession is not just saying, "I'm sorry." It is openly admitting, "I did it." Whether you need help from other people or just the accountability of walking in the light before God, pray the following prayer **aloud**:

> *Dear Heavenly Father, You have told me to put on the Lord Jesus Christ and make no provision for the flesh in regard to its lust. I confess that I have given in to fleshly lusts that wage war against my soul. I thank You that in Christ my sins are already forgiven, but I have broken Your holy law and I have allowed sin to wage war in my body. I come to You now to confess and renounce these sins of the flesh so that I might be cleansed and set free from the bondage of sin. Please reveal to my mind all the sins of the flesh I have committed and the ways I have grieved the Holy Spirit. In Jesus' holy name I pray. Amen.* [See Romans 6:12-13; 13:14; 2 Corinthians 4:2; James 4:1; 1 Peter 2:11; 5:8.]

The following list contains many sins of the flesh, but a prayerful examination of Mark 7:20-23; Galatians 5:19-21; Ephesians 4:25-31 and other Scripture passages will help you to be even more thorough. Look over the list below and the Scriptures just listed, and ask the Holy Spirit to bring to your mind the sins you need to confess. He may reveal others to you as well. For each one the Lord shows you, pray a prayer of confession from your heart. There is a sample prayer following the list. (**Note:** Sexual sins, eating disorders, substance abuse, abortion, suicidal tendencies and perfectionism will be dealt with later in this step. Further counseling may be necessary to find complete healing and freedom in these and other areas.)

❑ Stealing	❑ Swearing	❑ Cheating
❑ Quarreling/fighting	❑ Drunkenness	❑ Procrastination
❑ Jealousy/envy	❑ Lying	❑ Greed/materialism
❑ Gossip/slander	❑ Hatred	❑ Others:
❑ Sarcasm	❑ Anger	_____
❑ Lustful actions	❑ Lustful thoughts	_____
❑ Complaining/ criticism	❑ Apathy/ laziness	_____
		_____

Lord Jesus, I confess that I have sinned against You by [name the sins]. *Thank You for Your forgiveness and cleansing. I now turn away from these expressions of sin and turn to You, Lord. Fill me with Your Holy Spirit so that I will not carry out the desires of the flesh. In Jesus' name I pray. Amen.*

Note: If you are struggling with habitual sin, read Neil T. Anderson and Mike Quarles, *Overcoming Addictive Behavior* (Ventura, CA: Regal Books, 2003).

RESOLVING SEXUAL SIN

It is our responsibility not to allow sin to reign (rule) in our mortal bodies. We must not use our bodies or another person's body as an instrument of unrighteousness (see Romans 6:12-13). Sexual immorality is not only a sin against God but also it is a sin against your body, the temple of the Holy Spirit (see 1 Corinthians 6:18-19). To find freedom from sexual bondage, begin by praying the following prayer:

Lord Jesus, I have allowed sin to reign in my mortal body. I ask You to bring to my mind every sexual use of my body as an instrument of unrighteousness so that I can renounce these sexual sins and break those sinful bondages. In Jesus' name I pray. Amen.

As the Lord brings to your mind every immoral sexual use of your body, whether it was done to you (rape, incest, sexual molestation) or willingly by you (pornography, masturbation, sexual immorality), renounce every experience by saying the following prayer:

Lord Jesus, I renounce [name the sexual experience] with [name]. I ask You to break that sinful bond with [name] spiritually, physically and emotionally.

After you are finished, commit your body to the Lord by praying:

Lord Jesus, I renounce all these uses of my body as an instrument of unrighteousness, and I admit to any willful participation. I choose to present my physical body to You as an instrument of righteousness, a living and holy sacrifice, acceptable to You. I choose to reserve the sexual use of my body for marriage only. I reject the devil's lie that my body is not clean or that it is dirty or in any way unacceptable to You as a result of my past sexual experiences. Lord, thank You that You have cleansed and forgiven me and that You love and accept me just the way I am. Therefore, I choose now to accept myself and my body as clean in Your eyes. In Jesus' name I pray. Amen.

PRAYERS FOR SPECIFIC ISSUES

Pornography

Lord Jesus, I confess that I have looked at sexually suggestive and pornographic material for the purpose of stimulating myself sexually. I have attempted to satisfy my lustful desires and polluted my body, soul and spirit. Thank You for cleansing me and for Your forgiveness. I renounce any satanic bonds I have allowed in my life through the unrighteous use of my body and mind. Lord, I commit myself to destroy any objects in my possession that I have used for sexual stimulation, and to turn away from all media that are associated with my sexual sin. I commit myself to the renewing of my mind and to thinking pure thoughts. Fill me with Your Holy Spirit so that I may not carry out the desires of the flesh. In Jesus' name I pray. Amen.

Homosexuality

Lord Jesus, I renounce the lie that You have created me or anyone else to be homosexual, and I agree that in Your Word You clearly forbid homosexual behavior. I choose to accept myself as a child of God and I thank You that You created me as a man [woman]. I renounce all homosexual thoughts, urges, drives and acts, and I renounce all ways that Satan has used these things to pervert my relationships. I announce that I am free in Christ to relate to the opposite sex and my own sex in the way that You intended. In Jesus' name I pray. Amen.

Abortion

Lord Jesus, I confess that I was not a proper guardian and keeper of the life You entrusted to me, and I confess that I have sinned. Thank You that because of

Your forgiveness, I can forgive myself. I commit the child to You for all eternity and believe that he or she is in Your caring hands. In Jesus' name I pray. Amen.

Suicidal Tendencies

Lord Jesus, I renounce all suicidal thoughts and any attempts I've made to take my own life or in any way injure myself. I renounce the lie that life is hopeless and that I can find peace and freedom by taking my own life. Satan is a thief and comes to steal, kill and destroy. I choose life in Christ, who said He came to give me life and give it abundantly [see John 10:10]. *Thank You for Your forgiveness that allows me to forgive myself. I choose to believe that there is always hope in Christ and that my heavenly Father loves me. In Jesus' name I pray. Amen.*

Drivenness and Perfectionism

Lord Jesus, I renounce the lie that my sense of worth is dependent on my ability to perform. I announce the truth that my identity and my sense of worth are found in who I am as Your child. I renounce seeking the approval and acceptance of other people, and I choose to believe that I am already approved and accepted in Christ because of His death and resurrection for me. I choose to believe the truth that I have been saved, not by deeds done in righteousness, but according to Your mercy. I choose to believe that I am no longer under the curse of the Law because Christ became a curse for me. I receive the free gift of life in Christ and choose to abide in Him. I renounce striving for perfection by living under the Law. By Your grace, Heavenly Father, I choose from this day forward to walk by faith in the power of Your Holy Spirit according to what You have said is true. In Jesus' name I pray. Amen.

Eating Disorders or Self-Mutilation

Lord Jesus, I renounce the lie that my value as a person is dependent on my appearance or performance. I renounce cutting or abusing myself, vomiting, using laxatives or starving myself as a means of being in control, altering my appearance or trying to cleanse myself of evil. I announce that only the blood of the Lord Jesus Christ cleanses me from sin. I realize I have been bought with a price and my body, the temple of the Holy Spirit, belongs to God. Therefore, I choose to glorify God in my body. I renounce the lie that I am evil or that any part of my body is evil. Thank You that You accept me just the way I am in Christ. In Jesus' name I pray. Amen.

Substance Abuse

Lord Jesus, I confess that I have misused substances [alcohol, tobacco, food, prescription or street drugs] *for the purpose of pleasure, to escape reality or to cope with difficult problems. I confess that I have abused my body and programmed my mind in harmful ways. I have quenched the Holy Spirit as well. Thank You for Your forgiveness. I renounce any satanic connection or influence in my life through my misuse of food or chemicals. I cast my anxieties on Christ who loves me. I commit myself to yield no longer to substance abuse, but instead I choose to allow the Holy Spirit to direct and empower me. In Jesus' name I pray. Amen.*

OVERCOMING FEAR

Fear is a God-given natural response when our physical or psychological safety is threatened. Courage is not the absence of fear, but it is living by faith and doing what is right in the face of illegitimate fear objects. The fear of God is the beginning of wisdom and the only fear that can overcome all other fears. Irrational fears compel us to live irresponsible lives or prevent us from doing that which is responsible and from being good witnesses. Behind every irrational fear is a lie that must be identified. Allow the Lord to surface any controlling fears in your life and any root lies by praying the following prayer:

Dear Heavenly Father, I confess that I have allowed fear to control me and that lack of faith is sin. Thank You for Your forgiveness. I recognize that You have not given me a spirit of fear, but of power, love and discipline [see 2 Timothy 1:7]. I renounce any spirit of fear operating in my life and ask You to reveal any and all controlling fears in my life and the lies behind them. I desire to live by faith in You and in the power of the Holy Spirit. In Jesus' name I pray. Amen.

❑ Fear of death

❑ Fear of never loving or being loved

❑ Fear of Satan

❑ Fear of embarrassment

❑ Fear of failure

❑ Fear of being victimized

❑ Fear of rejection by other people

❑ Fear of marriage

❑ Fear of disapproval

❑ Fear of divorce

❑ Fear of becoming/being homosexual

❑ Fear of going crazy

❑ Fear of financial problems

❑ Fear of pain/illness

❑ Fear of never getting married

❑ Fear of the future

❑ Fear of the death of a loved one

❑ Fear of confrontation

❑ Fear of being a hopeless case

❑ Fear of specific individuals (List them.)

_____

_____

_____

_____

_____

_____

- ❏ Fear of losing my salvation

- ❏ Fear of not being loved by God

- ❏ Fear of having committed the
   unpardonable sin

- ❏ Other specific fears that come to mind:

  _____

  _____

  _____

  _____

Analyze Your Fear

When did you first experience the fear, and what events preceded the first experience? What lies have you been believing that are the basis for the fear? How has the fear kept you from living a responsible life or compromised your witness? Confess any active or passive way that you have allowed fear to control you. Work out a plan of responsible behavior, and determine in advance what your response will be to any fear object. Commit yourself to follow through with your plan. If you do the thing you fear the most, the death of fear is certain.

Lord Jesus, I renounce the fear of [name the fear and associated lies] *because God has not given me a spirit of fear. I choose to live by faith in You, and I acknowledge You as the only legitimate fear object in my life. In Jesus' name I pray. Amen.*

Note: For additional help with fear, read Neil T. Anderson and Rich Miller, *Freedom from Fear* (Eugene, OR: Harvest House Publishers, 1999).

STEP 7

CURSES VERSUS BLESSINGS

Scripture declares that the iniquities of one generation can be visited on the third and fourth generations, but God's blessings will be poured out on thousands of generations of those who love and obey Him (see Exodus 20:4-6).

The iniquities of one generation can adversely affect future ones unless those sins are renounced, and your new spiritual heritage in Christ is claimed. This cycle of abuse and all negative influences can be stopped through genuine repentance. Jesus died for your sins, but that is only appropriated when you choose to believe Him and only experienced when you repent. You are not guilty of your ancestors' sins, but because of their sins you have been affected by their influence. Jesus said that after we have been fully trained we will be like our teachers (see Luke 6:40), and Peter wrote that you were redeemed "from your futile way of life inherited from your forefathers" (1 Peter 1:18). Ask the Lord to reveal your ancestral sins and then renounce them as follows:

> *Dear Heavenly Father, please reveal to my mind all the sins of my ancestors that have been passed down through family lines. Since I am a new creation in Christ, I want to experience my freedom from these influences and walk in my new identity as a child of God. In Jesus' name I pray. Amen.*

> *Lord, I renounce* [confess all the family sins that God brings to your mind].

Satan and people may curse us, but it will not have any effect on us unless we believe it. We cannot passively take our place in Christ—we must actively and intentionally choose to submit to God and to resist the devil, and then the devil will flee from us. Complete this final step with the following declaration and prayer:

Declaration: *I here and now reject and disown all the sins of my ancestors. As one who has been delivered from the domain of darkness and transferred into the kingdom of God's Son, I declare myself to be free from those harmful influences. I am no longer "in Adam." I am now alive "in Christ." Therefore, I am the recipient of the blessings of God upon my life as I choose to love and obey Him. As one who has been crucified and raised with Christ and who sits with Him in heavenly places, I renounce any and all satanic* *attacks and assignments directed against me and my ministry. Every curse placed on me was broken when Christ became a curse for me by dying on the cross* [see Galatians 3:13]. *I reject any and every way in which Satan may claim ownership of me. I belong to the Lord Jesus Christ who purchased me with His own precious blood. I declare myself to be fully and eternally signed over and committed to the Lord Jesus Christ. Therefore, having submitted to God and by His authority, I now resist the devil, and I command every spiritual enemy of the Lord Jesus Christ to leave my presence. I put on the armor of God and I stand against Satan's temptations, accusations and deceptions. From this day forward I will seek to do only the will of my heavenly Father.*

Prayer: *Dear Heavenly Father, I come to You as Your child, bought out of slavery to sin by the blood of the Lord Jesus Christ. You are the Lord of the universe and the Lord of my life. I submit my body to You as a living and holy sacrifice. May You be glorified through my life and body. I now ask You to fill me with Your Holy Spirit. I commit myself to the renewing of my mind in order that I may prove that Your will is good, acceptable and perfect for me. I desire nothing more than to be like You. I pray, believe and do all this in the wonderful name of Jesus, my Lord and Savior. Amen.*

MAINTAINING YOUR FREEDOM

It is exciting to experience your freedom in Christ, but what you have gained must be maintained. You have won an important battle, but the war goes on. To maintain your freedom in Christ and grow in the grace of God, you must continue renewing your mind according to the truth of God's Word. If you become aware of lies that you have believed, renounce them and choose the truth. If more painful memories surface, then forgive those who hurt you and renounce any sinful part you played. Many people choose to go through the Steps again on their own to make sure they have dealt with all their issues. Oftentimes new issues will surface. The process can assist you when you do a regular housecleaning.

It is not uncommon after going though the Steps to Freedom in Christ for people to have thoughts such as *Nothing has really changed; I'm the same person I always was* or *It didn't work*. In most cases you should just ignore these thoughts. We are not called to dispel the darkness; we are called to turn on the light. You don't get rid of negative thoughts by rebuking every one; you get rid of them by repenting and choosing the truth.

I encourage you to read the books *Victory Over the Darkness* and *The Bondage Breaker* if you haven't already done so in preparation for going through the Steps. The 21-day devotional *Walking in Freedom* was written for those who have completed the Steps.[1] If you want to continue growing in the grace of God, I also suggest the following:

- Get rid of or destroy any cult or occult objects in your home (see Acts 19:18-20).

- Get involved in a small-group ministry where you can be a real person, and be part of a church where God's truth is taught with kindness and grace.

- Read and meditate on the truth of God's Word each day.

- Don't let your mind be passive, especially concerning what you watch and listen to (music, TV, etc.). Actively take every thought captive to the obedience of Christ.

- Learn to pray by the Spirit (for information, read *Praying by the Power of the Spirit*).[2]

- Remember, you are responsible for your mental, spiritual and physical health (for more information on the latter, read *The Biblical Guide to Alternative Medicine*).[3]

- Work through the *Freedom in Christ Bible*, a discipleship study Bible that takes you through the sanctifying process five days a week for a year.[4]

DAILY PRAYER AND DECLARATION

Dear Heavenly Father, I praise You and honor You as my Lord and Savior. You are in control of all things. I thank You that You are always with me and will never leave me nor forsake me. You are the only all-powerful and only wise God. You are kind and loving in all Your ways. I love You and thank You that I am united with Christ and spiritually alive in Him. I choose not to love the world or the things in the world, and I crucify the flesh and all its passions.

Thank You for the life I now have in Christ. I ask You to fill me with the Holy Spirit so that I can be guided by You and not carry out the desires of the flesh. I declare my total dependence on You, and I take my stand against Satan and all his lying ways. I choose to believe the truth of God's Word despite what my feelings may say. I refuse to be discouraged; You are the God of all hope. Nothing is too difficult for You. I am confident that You will supply all my needs as I seek to live according to Your Word. I thank You that I can be content and live a responsible life through Christ who strengthens me.

I now take my stand against Satan and command him and all his evil spirits to depart from me. I choose to put on the full armor of God so that I may be able to stand firm against all the devil's schemes. I submit my body as a living and holy sacrifice to You, and I choose to renew my mind by Your living Word. By so doing I will be able to prove that Your will is good, acceptable and perfect for me. In the name of my Lord and Savior, Jesus Christ, I pray. Amen.

BEDTIME PRAYER

Thank You, Lord, that You have brought me into Your family and have blessed me with every spiritual blessing in the heavenly places in Christ Jesus. Thank You for this time of renewal and refreshment through sleep. I accept it as one of Your blessings for Your children, and I trust You to guard my mind and my body during my sleep.

As I have thought about You and Your truth during the day, I choose to let those good thoughts continue in my mind while I am asleep. I commit myself to You for Your protection against every attempt of Satan and his demons to attack me during sleep. Guard my mind from nightmares. I renounce all fear and cast every anxiety upon You, Lord. I commit myself to You as my rock, my fortress and my strong tower. May Your peace be upon this place of rest. In the strong name of the Lord Jesus Christ I pray. Amen.

PRAYER FOR SPIRITUAL CLEANSING OF HOME, APARTMENT OR ROOM

After removing and destroying all objects of false worship, pray this prayer **aloud** in every room:

Heavenly Father, I acknowledge that You are the Lord of heaven and Earth. In Your sovereign power and love, You have entrusted me with many things. Thank You for this place to live. I claim my home as a place of spiritual safety for me and my family and ask for Your protection from all the attacks of the enemy. As a child of God, raised up and seated with Christ in the heavenly places, I command every evil spirit claiming ground in this place, based on the activities of past or present occupants, including me and my family, to leave and never return. I renounce all demonic assignments directed against this place. I ask You, Heavenly Father, to post Your holy angels around this place to guard it from any and all attempts of the enemy to enter and disturb Your purposes for me and my family. I thank You, Lord, for doing this in the name of the Lord Jesus Christ. Amen.

PRAYER FOR LIVING IN A NON-CHRISTIAN ENVIRONMENT

After removing and destroying all objects of false worship in your possession, pray this **aloud** in the place where you live:

Thank You, Heavenly Father, for a place to live and to be renewed by sleep. I ask You to set aside my room [or portion of this room] *as a place of spiritual safety for me. I renounce any allegiance given to false gods or spirits by other occupants. I renounce any claim to this room* [space] *by Satan based on the activities of past or present occupants, including me. On the basis of my position as a child of God and joint heir with Christ, who has all authority in heaven and on Earth, I command all evil spirits to leave this place and never return. I ask You, Heavenly Father, to station Your holy angels to protect me while I live here. In Jesus' mighty name I pray. Amen.*

Paul prays in Ephesians 1:18, "I pray that the eyes of your heart may be enlightened, so that you will know what is the hope of His calling, what are the riches of the glory of His inheritance in the saints, and what is the surpassing greatness of His power toward us who believe." Beloved, you are a child of God (see 1 John 3:1-3), and "My God will supply all your needs according to His riches in glory in Christ Jesus" (Philippians 4:19). The critical needs are the "being" needs such as eternal or spiritual life that He has given you and the identity that you have in Christ. In addition, Jesus has met your needs for *acceptance, security* and *significance*. Memorize and meditate on the following truths daily. Read the entire list **aloud**, morning and evening, for the next few weeks. Think about what you are reading and let the truth of who you are in Christ renew your mind. This is your inheritance in Christ.

IN CHRIST

I renounce the lie that I am rejected, unloved or shameful. In Christ I am accepted. God says that:

- I am God's child [see John 1:12].
- I am Christ's friend [see John 15:5].
- I have been justified [see Romans 5:1].
- I am united with the Lord, and I am one spirit with Him [see 1 Corinthians 6:17].
- I have been bought with a price. I belong to God [see 1 Corinthians 6:19-20].
- I am a member of Christ's Body [see 1 Corinthians 12:27].
- I am a saint, a holy one [see Ephesians 1:1].
- I have been adopted as God's child [see Ephesians 1:5].
- I have direct access to God through the Holy Spirit [see Ephesians 2:18].
- I have been redeemed and forgiven of all my sins [see Colossians 1:14].
- I am complete in Christ [see Colossians 2:10].

I renounce the lie that I am guilty, unprotected, alone or abandoned. In Christ *I am secure.* God says that:

- I am free from condemnation [see Romans 8:1-2].
- I am assured that all things work together for good [see Romans 8:28].
- I am free from any condemning charges against me [see Romans 8:31-34].
- I cannot be separated from the love of God [see Romans 8:35-39].
- I have been established, anointed and sealed by God [see 2 Corinthians 1:21-22].

- I am confident the good work that God has begun in me will be perfected [see Philippians 1:6].

- I am a citizen of heaven [see Philippians 3:20].

- I am hidden with Christ in God [see Colossians 3:3].

- I have not been given a spirit of fear but of power, love and discipline [see 2 Timothy 1:7].

- I can find grace and mercy to help in time of need [see Hebrews 4:16].

- I am born of God and the evil one cannot touch me [see 1 John 5:18].

I renounce the lie that I am worthless, inadequate, helpless or hopeless. In Christ *I am significant*. God says that:

- I am the salt of the earth and the light of the world [see Matthew 5:13-14].
- I am a branch of the true vine, Jesus, a channel of His life [see John 15:1,5].
- I have been chosen and appointed by God to bear fruit [see John 15:16].
- I am a personal, Spirit-empowered witness of Christ's [see Acts 1:8].
- I am a temple of God [see 1 Corinthians 3:16].
- I am a minister of reconciliation for God [see 2 Corinthians 5:17-21].
- I am God's coworker [see 2 Corinthians 6:1].
- I am seated with Christ in the heavenly realm [see Ephesians 2:6].
- I am God's workmanship, created for good works [see Ephesians 2:10].
- I may approach God with freedom and confidence [see Ephesians 3:12].
- I can do all things through Christ who strengthens me [see Philippians 4:13]!

I AM NOT THE GREAT "I AM,"
BUT BY THE GRACE OF GOD I AM WHO I AM.
[See Exodus 3:14; John 8:24,28,58; 1 Corinthians 15:10.]

Notes
1. Neil T. Anderson, *Walking in Freedom* (Ventura, CA: Regal Books, 1999).
2. Neil T. Anderson, *Praying by the Power of the Spirit* (Eugene, OR: Harvest House, 2003).
3. Neil T. Anderson and Michael Jacobson, *The Biblical Guide to Alternative Medicine* (Ventura, CA: Regal Books, 2003).
4. Neil T. Anderson, gen. ed., *Freedom in Christ Bible* (Grand Rapids, MI: Zondervan Publishing House, 2001).

GODLY RELATIONSHIPS

AND HE SAID TO HIM, "'YOU SHALL LOVE THE LORD YOUR GOD WITH
ALL YOUR HEART, AND WITH ALL YOUR SOUL, AND WITH ALL YOUR MIND.'
THIS IS THE GREAT AND FOREMOST COMMANDMENT. THE SECOND IS LIKE IT,
'YOU SHALL LOVE YOUR NEIGHBOR AS YOURSELF.' ON THESE TWO
COMMANDMENTS DEPEND THE WHOLE LAW AND THE PROPHETS."
MATTHEW 22:37-40

WORD

In this session we will consider rights, responsibilities, judgment, discipline, accountability and the needs of others. The great commandment says we are to love the Lord our God with all our hearts, souls and minds, and to love our neighbor as ourselves (see Matthew 22:37-39). This sums up the whole biblical message—we are called to fall in love with God *and* with one another. A right relationship with God should lead to a right relationship with our neighbors.

RIGHTS AND RESPONSIBILITIES

Have you ever listened to a couple caught in a vicious argument? Inevitably each partner starts ripping the other's character while looking out for his or her own needs. Nobody can have good relationships with that orientation. If you want to get a biblical orientation to relationships, read the following Scripture passages:

- Romans 14:4

- Philippians 2:3-5

- 1 John 4:19-21

Figure 10-A

BEING AWARE OF OUR OWN SINS

- **Moses** (Exodus 33:18). When Moses prayed "Show me Your glory" (Exodus 33:18), he was asking for a manifestation of God's presence. In answer to Moses, God placed him in the cleft of a rock and His glory passed behind him. The experience was so profound that Moses' face radiated the glory of God for days.

- **Isaiah** (Isaiah 6:5). Isaiah had a similar experience, and when he did, he exclaimed, "Woe is me, for I am ruined! Because I am a man of unclean lips, and I live among a people of unclean lips; for my eyes have seen the King, the Lord of hosts" (Isaiah 6:5).

- **Peter** (Luke 5:3-8). In Luke 5:3, Jesus approached Peter who had been fishing all night without success. Jesus said to him, "Put into the deep water and let down your nets for a catch" (v. 4). Peter obediently went back to the sea and started pulling in fish. He must have suddenly realized that someone very special was in the boat with him—someone who could command even the fish—and he responded, "Go away from me, Lord, for I am a sinful man" (v. 8).

A. Discipline Versus Judgment

   1. **Discipline** (see Hebrews 12:5-11). God's discipline is a proof of His love. In fact, if we are not at times disciplined by God, then we are illegitimate children of God.

2. **Judgment.** Judgment is not the same as discipline. Judgment is related to character, whereas discipline is related to behavior.

B. Discipline Versus Punishment
There is also a major difference between discipline and punishment. Punishment is related to the Old Testament concept of an eye for an eye. Punishment is retroactive, whereas discipline is future oriented.

Learning Not to Be Defensive (1 Peter 2:23)

A. Shame, Guilt, Grace
Many cultures in the world are shame based. In these cultures, people are ashamed of themselves when it is perceived that there is something wrong with them. Legalistic churches can make people feel guilty whenever they don't measure up to the expectations of the church. Under the law, people feel guilty when they have done something wrong. Christianity is grace based. Under the grace of God, we are new creations in Christ, and we are no longer under the law.

B. Authority and Accountability (1 Thessalonians 2:5-8)
God has established lines of authority. Had He not done so, there would be nothing but anarchy in society. We also have a great need for accountability. Which of the following steps of authority best describes how the Lord came to you?

List A	List B
1. Authority	1. Acceptance
2. Accountability	2. Affirmation
3. Affirmation	3. Accountability
4. Acceptance	4. Authority

Expressing Our Needs (Luke 6:38; Titus 3:14)

When pressing needs are not being met, it is important that we let people know about those needs. It is prideful to let others assume that we have no needs or refuse to share our needs with others.

One of Life's Little Secrets

One of life's great compensations is that we cannot sincerely help another without helping ourselves in the process. Read the following poem:

ANYWAY

People are unreasonable, illogical and self-centered.
Love them anyway.
If you do good, people will accuse you
of selfish, ulterior motives.
Do good anyway.
If you are successful, you will win
false friends and true enemies.
Succeed anyway.
The good you do today will be forgotten tomorrow.
Do good anyway.
Honesty and frankness make you vulnerable.
Be honest and frank anyway.
The biggest people with the biggest ideas can be shot down by the smallest
people with the smallest minds.
Think big anyway.
People favor underdogs but follow only top dogs.
Fight for the underdog anyway.
What you spend years building
may be destroyed overnight.
Build anyway.
People really need help, but may
attack you if you help them.
Help people anyway.
Give the world the best you've got and you'll get kicked in the teeth.
Give the world the best you've got anyway.

Each of us can be the kind of person God created us to be in spite of others and
the sad philosophies of this fallen world.

WITNESS

1. Being an ambassador for Christ and having a positive witness are directly
   related to our capacity to love others. How can you be a good neighbor to
   those who live on your street; i.e., how can you love your neighbor as yourself?

2. What needs do your neighbors have that you could help meet?

3. How could you get to know your neighbors better so that you would have a better idea of what their needs are?

4. What needs do you share in common with your neighbors?

DISCUSSION QUESTIONS

1. What is your responsibility concerning yourself and your neighbors?

2. Why do people have a tendency to judge others and look out for their own needs?

3. If you become critical of others and unaware of your own sins, what is the problem and what can you do about it?

4. Why shouldn't we be another person's conscience? What will happen if we try to be?

5. What happens if we emphasize rights over responsibilities?

6. What is the difference between judgment and discipline?

7. What is the difference between discipline and punishment?

8. Should you be defensive if someone attacks your character? Why or why not?

9. Share a personal experience when an authority figure demanded accountability without affirmation and acceptance. How did you respond to that person? How will knowing this affect your ministry or parenting?

10. How can we share a need without its backfiring on us?

TAKING IT WITH YOU

SUGGESTIONS FOR QUIET TIME

During the coming week, read Luke 6:27-42 and think about how you relate to your family, friends and neighbors. Search your heart and ask the Holy Spirit to reveal anyone from whom you should seek forgiveness. If anyone comes to mind, go to that person and state clearly what you have done wrong; then ask for forgiveness. (**Note:** Don't write a letter that can be misunderstood or used against you.)

THE BIG QUESTION

Before the next session, consider the following question: How can you set goals for your life that are consistent with God's will?

GOALS AND DESIRES

BUT THE GOAL OF OUR INSTRUCTION IS LOVE FROM A PURE
HEART AND A GOOD CONSCIENCE AND A SINCERE FAITH.
1 TIMOTHY 1:5

WORD

God's goals for our lives are definable, defensible and achievable by faith. We must learn to differentiate between godly goals and personal desires. If we have the wrong goals, the results will show up in the way we live. Wrong goals can be blocked (resulting in anger), uncertain (resulting in anxiety) and impossible (leading to depression).

LIVING ON THE RIGHT PATH

Our Christian walk is the result of what we believe. If our faith is off, our walk will be off. If our walk is off, we need to take a good look at what we believe. Walking by faith simply means functioning in daily life on the basis of what we believe. In fact, we are already walking by faith—every person alive is. The difference is in what (or whom) we believe. If what we are doing is no longer bearing any fruit, we need to change what we believe, because our misbehavior is the result of what we have chosen to believe.

FEELINGS ARE GOD'S RED FLAGS OF WARNING

A. Anger Signals a Blocked Goal
    When activity in a relationship or a project results in feelings of anger, it is usually because someone or something has prevented us from accomplishing what we wanted.

B. Anxiety Signals an Uncertain Goal

When we feel anxious in a task or a relationship, this can be a signal that we are uncertain about our goal.

C. Depression Signals an Impossible Goal

Depression can be the result of biochemical factors; but if there is no physical cause, then depression is often rooted in a sense of hopelessness or helplessness. This type of depression is a signal that a particular goal, no matter how spiritual or noble, may be impossible or hopeless.

WRONG RESPONSES TO THOSE WHO FRUSTRATE GOALS

When someone or something threatens our plans, some of us may attempt to control or manipulate the people or circumstances that stand between us and our goals; or respond by getting bitter, angry or resentful; or maybe even resort to playing the martyr.

TURNING BAD GOALS INTO GOOD GOALS

God does not assign goals that we can't achieve. His goals are possible, certain and achievable. We need to understand what His goals for our lives are and then say as Mary said: "Behold, the bondslave of the Lord; be it done to me according to your word" (Luke 1:38).

GOALS VERSUS DESIRES

A **godly goal** is any specific orientation that reflects God's purpose for our life and does not depend on people or circumstances beyond our ability or right to control. A **godly desire** is any specific result that depends on the cooperation of other people or on the success of events or favorable circumstances, which we have no right or ability to control.

GOD'S PRIMARY GOAL FOR US

God's goal for us is that we become who He created us to be. Sanctification is God's will—His goal—for our life (see 1 Thessalonians 4:3). There are distractions, diversions, disappointments, trials, temptations and traumas that come along to disrupt the process; however, the tribulations we face are actually a means of achieving the supreme goal of conforming to the image of God. Read the following poem by an unknown author:

"Disappointments—His appointment,"
Change one letter, then I see
That the thwarting of my purpose
Is God's better choice for me.
His appointment must be blessing,
Tho' it may come in disguise,
For the end from the beginning
Open to His wisdom lies.

"Disappointment—His appointment,"
No good will He withhold,
From denials oft we gather
treasures of His love untold.
Well He knows each broken purpose
Leads to fuller, deeper trust,
And the end of all His dealings
Proves our God is wise and just.

"Disappointments—His appointment,"
Lord, I take it, then, as such,
Like clay in hands of a potter,
Yielding wholly to Thy touch.
My life's plan is Thy molding;
Not one single choice be mine;
Let me answer, unrepining
"Father, not my will, but Thine."

WITNESS

How can distinguishing between goals and desires make you a better witness?

DISCUSSION QUESTIONS

1. If goals and desires are something you adopt in your own mind, how can you know emotionally if you are in the center of God's will?

2. How does the world typically respond to blocked goals? What has been your typical response?

3. Why is a manipulator or controller insecure? What false beliefs is such a person harboring?

4. What is God's primary goal for your life? Why can't that goal be blocked?

5. How does the fruit of the Spirit demonstrate the antithesis of false goals?

6. How does a Christian establish a legitimate sense of worth?

7. How can you live so that you never stumble, and if you aren't living that way, what should you do about it?

SUGGESTIONS FOR QUIET TIME

This coming week, take the time to evaluate your faith by completing the following Faith Appraisal. Circle the number that best describes your answer to each question; then complete the sentence that follows each question. (**Note:** You will *not* be asked to share your results with the group. This is a self-appraisal to help you evaluate your own faith.)

	Low				High
1. How successful am I? I would be more successful if . . .	1	2	3	4	5
2. How significant am I? I would be more significant if . . .	1	2	3	4	5
3. How fulfilled am I? I would be more fulfilled if . . .	1	2	3	4	5

4. How satisfied am I?   1   2   3   4   5
   I would be more satisfied if . . .

5. How happy am I?   1   2   3   4   5
   I would be happier if . . .

6. How much fun am I having?   1   2   3   4   5
   I would have more fun if . . .

7. How secure am I?   1   2   3   4   5
   I would be more secure if . . .

8. How peaceful am I?   1   2   3   4   5
   I would have more peace if . . .

THE BIG QUESTION

Before the next session, consider the following question:

If you discover that your goals are not the same as God's goals for your life, what will you need to do to change your focus?

LIVING ON THE RIGHT PATH

NOT THAT I SPEAK FROM WANT, FOR I HAVE LEARNED TO BE CONTENT IN WHATEVER CIRCUMSTANCES I AM. I KNOW HOW TO GET ALONG WITH HUMBLE MEANS, AND I ALSO KNOW HOW TO LIVE IN PROSPERITY; IN ANY AND EVERY CIRCUMSTANCE I HAVE LEARNED THE SECRET OF BEING FILLED AND GOING HUNGRY, BOTH OF HAVING ABUNDANCE AND SUFFER-ING NEED. I CAN DO ALL THINGS THROUGH HIM WHO STRENGTHENS ME.
PHILIPPIANS 4:11-13

WORD

Each of us lives by faith. We must examine what we believe and renew our minds to the truth of God's Word if we are going to be successful, fulfilled, satisfied and content. In this last session we will examine what we believe in light of God's Word concerning eight aspects of our personal life.

GOD'S GUIDELINES FOR THE WALK OF FAITH

A. Success (Key Concept: Goals)
   Success is accepting God's goals for our lives and, by His grace, becoming what He has called us to be (see Joshua 1:7-8; 2 Peter 1:3-10; 3 John 2).

B. Significance (Key Concept: Time)
   What is forgotten in the passing of time is of little significance. What is remembered for eternity is of greatest significance (see Acts 5:33-40; 1 Corinthians 3:13; 1 Timothy 4:7-8).

C. Fulfillment (Key Concept: Role Preference)
    Fulfillment is discovering our own uniqueness in Christ and using our gifts to build others up and glorify the Lord (see Matthew 25:14-30; Romans 12:1-18; 2 Timothy 4:5).

D. Satisfaction (Key Concept: Quality)
    Satisfaction is living righteously and seeking to raise the quality of the relationships, services and products with which we are involved (see Proverbs 18:24; Matthew 5:5; 2 Timothy 4:7).

E. Happiness (Key Concept: Wanting What You Have)
    Happiness is being thankful for what we have rather than focusing on what we don't have (see Philippians 4:12; 1 Thessalonians 5:18; 1 Timothy 6:6-8).

F. Fun (Key Concept: Uninhibited Spontaneity)
    The secret to fun is removing unbiblical blocks such as keeping up appearances (see 2 Samuel 6:20-22; Romans 14:22; Galatians 1:10; 5:1).

G. Security (Key Concept: Relating to the Eternal)
    Insecurity comes when we depend on things that will pass away rather than on things that will last forever (see John 10:27-29; Romans 8:31-39; Ephesians 1:13-14).

H. Peace (Key Concept: Establishing Internal Order)
    The peace of God is internal, not external (see Isaiah 32:17; Jeremiah 6:14; John 14:27; Philippians 4:6-7).

    • Peace on Earth is what we want.

    • Peace with God is something we already have.

    • Peace of God is something we need.

WITNESS

How can you be a good ambassador for Christ?

DISCUSSION QUESTIONS

1. How can a successful politician, businessperson or scientist live consistently with God's Word?

2. On what does your success as a Christian depend?

3. What does the world call "significant" that in light of eternity is really insignificant?

4. How can you live a more fulfilled life?

5. Can anything the flesh craves ever be satisfying?

6. What satisfies and continues to satisfy?

7. How can you truly be happy in this world?

8. How can you experience the joy of the Lord and make your Christian experience more fun?

9. What causes you to feel insecure?

10. How can you be more secure?

11. How do goals and desires relate to the possibility of experiencing peace?

12. What kind of peace can you have and how do you get it?

Books and Resources by
Dr. Neil T. Anderson

About Dr. Neil T. Anderson

Dr. Neil T. Anderson was formerly the chairman of the Practical Theology Department at Talbot School of Theology. In 1989, he founded Freedom in Christ Ministries, which now has staff and offices in various countries around the world. He is currently on the Freedom in Christ Ministries International Board, which oversees this global ministry. For more information about Dr. Anderson and his ministry, visit his website at www.ficminternational.org.

Core Message and Materials

Victory Over the Darkness with study guide, audiobook and DVD (Regal Books, 2000). With over 1,000,000 copies in print, this core book explains who you are in Christ, how to walk by faith in the power of the Holy Spirit, how to be transformed by the renewing of your mind, how to experience emotional freedom, and how to relate to one another in Christ.

The Bondage Breaker with study guide, audiobook (Harvest House Publishers, 2000) and DVD (Regal Books, 2006). With over 1,000,000 copies in print, this book explains spiritual warfare, what our protection is, ways that we are vulnerable, and how we can live a liberated life in Christ.

Discipleship Counseling with DVD (Regal Books, 2003). This book combines the concepts of discipleship and counseling and teaches the practical integration of theology and psychology for helping Christians resolve their personal and spiritual conflicts through repentance and faith in God.

Steps to Freedom in Christ and interactive videocassette (Regal Books, 2004). This discipleship counseling tool helps Christians resolve their personal and spiritual conflicts.

Helping Others Find Freedom in Christ DVD (Regal Books, 2007). In this DVD package, Neil explains the seven Steps to Freedom and how to apply them through discipleship counseling. He explains the biblical basis for the steps and helps viewers understand the root cause of personal and spiritual problems.

Beta: The Next Step in Your Journey with Christ (Regal Books, 2004) is a discipleship course for Sunday School classes and small groups. The kit includes a teacher's guide, a student guide and two DVDs covering 12 lessons and the Steps to Freedom in Christ. This course is designed to enable new and stagnant believers to resolve personal and spiritual conflicts and be established alive and free in Christ.

The Daily Discipler (Regal Books, 2005). This practical systematic theology is a culmination of all of Neil's books covering the major doctrines of the Christian faith and the problems they face. It is a five-day-per-week, one-year study that will thoroughly ground believers in their faith.

Restored (e3 Resources, 2007). This book illustrates and expands the Steps to Freedom in Christ, making it easier for an individual to process the Steps on his or her own.

Victory Over the Darkness Series

Overcoming a Negative Self-Image, with Dave Park (Regal, 2003)
Overcoming Addictive Behavior, with Mike Quarles (Regal, 2003)
Overcoming Doubt (Regal, 2004)
Overcoming Depression, with Joanne Anderson (Regal, 2004) and DVD (2007)

Bondage Breaker Series

Praying by the Power of the Spirit (Harvest House Publishers, 2003)

Finding God's Will in Spiritually Deceptive Times (Harvest House Publishers, 2003)

Finding Freedom in a Sex-Obsessed World (Harvest House Publishers, 2004)

Specialized Books

God's Power at Work in You, with Dr. Robert Saucy (Harvest House Publishers, 2001). A thorough analysis of sanctification and practical instruction on how we grow in Christ.

Released from Bondage, with Judith King and Dr. Fernando Garzon (Thomas Nelson, 2002). This book has personal accounts of defeated Christians with explanatory notes of how they resolved their conflicts and found their freedom in Christ, and how the message of Discipleship Counseling can be applied to therapy with research results.

Daily in Christ, with Joanne Anderson (Harvest House Publishers, 2000). This popular daily devotional is also being used by thousands of Internet subscribers every day.

Who I Am in Christ (Regal Books, 2001). In 36 short chapters, this book describes who you are in Christ and how He meets your deepest needs.

Freedom from Addiction, with Mike and Julia Quarles (Regal Books, 1997). Using Mike's testimony, this book explains the nature of chemical addictions and how to overcome them in Christ.

One Day at a Time, with Mike and Julia Quarles (Regal Books, 2000). This devotional helps those who struggle with addictive behaviors and explains how to discover the grace of God on a daily basis.

Freedom from Fear, with Rich Miller (Harvest House Publishers, 1999). This book explains anxiety disorders and how to overcome them.

Extreme Church Makeover, with Charles Mylander (Regal Books, 2006). This book offers guidelines and encouragement for resolving seemingly impossible corporate conflicts in the church and also provides leaders with a primary means for church growth—releasing the power of God in the church.

Experiencing Christ Together, with Dr. Charles Mylander (Regal Books, 2006.) This book explains God's divine plan for marriage and the steps that couples can take to resolve their difficulties.

Christ Centered Therapy, with Dr. Terry and Julie Zuehlke (Zondervan Publishing House, 2000). A textbook explaining the practical integration of theology and psychology for professional counselors.

Getting Anger Under Control, with Rich Miller (Harvest House Publishers, 1999). This book explains the basis for anger and how to control it.

The Biblical Guide to Alternative Medicine, with Dr. Michael Jacobson (Regal Books, 2003). This book develops a grid by which you can evaluate medical practices, and then applies the grid to the world's most recognized philosophies of medicine and health.

Breaking the Strongholds of Legalism, with Rich Miller and Paul Travis (Harvest House Publishers, 2003). An explanation of legalism and how to overcome it.

For more information, contact Freedom in Christ Ministries at the following:

Canada: freedominchrist@sasktel.net or www.ficm.ca
India: isactara@gmail.com
Switzerland: info@freiheitinchristus.ch or www.freiheitinchristus.ch
United Kingdom: info@ficm.org.uk or www.ficm.org.uk
United States: info@ficm.org or www.ficm.org
International: www.ficminternational.org
Dr. Anderson: www.discipleshipcounsel.com

Also visit
www.bethanyhouse.com